The Rise and Fall of *Capitalism*

Anthony Usher, D.Min.

TEACH Services, Inc.
PUBLISHING
www.TEACHServices.com • (800) 367-1844

World rights reserved. This book or any portion thereof may not be copied or reproduced in any form or manner whatever, except as provided by law, without the written permission of the publisher, except by a reviewer who may quote brief passages in a review.

The author assumes full responsibility for the accuracy of all facts and quotations as cited in this book. The opinions expressed in this book are the author's personal views and interpretations, and do not necessarily reflect those of the publisher.

This book is provided with the understanding that the publisher is not engaged in giving spiritual, legal, medical, or other professional advice. If authoritative advice is needed, the reader should seek the counsel of a competent professional.

Copyright © 2014 Anthony Usher
Copyright © 2014 TEACH Services, Inc.
ISBN-13: 978-1-4796-0305-3(Paperback)
ISBN-13: 978-1-4796-0306-0 (ePub)
ISBN-13: 978-1-4796-0307-7 (Mobi)
Library of Congress Control Number: 2014944905

All scripture quotations, unless otherwise marked, are taken from the New King James Version®. Copyright © 1982 by Thomas Nelson, Inc. Used by permission. All rights reserved.

Scripture quotations marked KJV are taken from the King James Version. Public domain.

Scripture quotations marked NASB are taken from the New American Standard Bible®, Copyright © 1960, 1962, 1968, 1971, 1972, 1973, 1975, 1977, 1995 by The Lockman Foundation. Used by permission.

Scripture quotations marked NIV are taken from the Holy Bible, New International Version®, NIV®. Copyright © 1973, 1978, 1984, 2011 by Biblica, Inc.™ Used by permission of Zondervan. All rights reserved worldwide.

Scripture quotations marked MSG are taken from *THE MESSAGE*. Copyright © by Eugene H. Peterson 1993, 1994, 1995, 1996, 2000, 2001, 2002. Used by permission of NavPress Publishing Group.

Published by

www.TEACHServices.com • (800) 367-1844

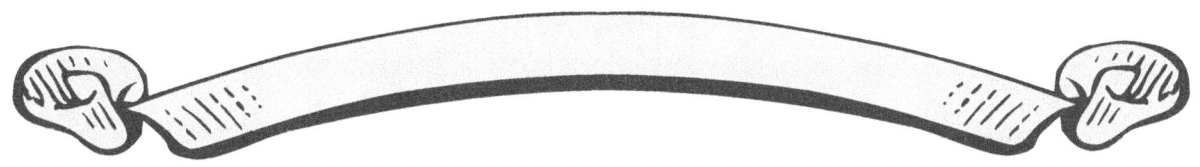

Contents

Chapter 1	An Introduction to the Scope of the Problem	5
Chapter 2	What Is Capitalism?	9
Chapter 3	A Brief History of Capitalism	17
Chapter 4	How Capitalism Perpetuates Poverty	27
Chapter 5	How Government Perpetuates Poverty	32
Chapter 6	The Poor Will Always Be With You	41
Chapter 7	Economic Recession: A Blessing in Disguise?	48
Chapter 8	The Decline of Capitalism: Part 1	52
Chapter 9	The Decline of Capitalism: Part 2	57
Chapter 10	The Decline of Capitalism: Part 3	62
Chapter 11	The Economic Utopia	67
Chapter 12	Religious-Political Issues	73
Chapter 13	The Arab-Israeli Conflict	80

Chapter 14	The Fifth World Empire	90
Chapter 15	The Fall of Capitalism	98
Bibliography		103

Dedication

In affection and gratitude, this book is dedicated to the loving memory of both my deceased parents: Eileen Estella and Reginald Emmanuel Beckett Usher who fought against all odds and whose unconditional love pushed me to do the impossible and to become all that I could be. In life they never gave up and in death, they await the resurrection morning.

To my darling wife Laurene and our three sons—
Arlington, Erick, and Warner—who silently sacrificed so much of their time.
They were the wind beneath my wings.

To all my surviving siblings: Allan, Reginald Jr., Lucille, Arthur, George, Norman, Gilroy, Earl, and Rose Marie, who are dreaming their version of the American Dream at night, but wake up to live it in the morning.

Finally, to all those working for a pittance of a salary,
without health care benefits, and with no exit sign in sight at the end of the
long, dark tunnel of capitalistic enslavement; this book is dedicated
to you as a stubborn reminder that we shall overcome; someday.

Chapter 1

the Problem

American politics has been my obsession for the past two decades. The partisan manner with which sensitive socio-religious political issues (welfare, social security, unemployment, wages, health care, immigration, Wall Street, environmental abuse, lesbian, gay, bisexual and transgender (LGBT) relationships, abortion, and the Arab-Israeli conflict) have been handled has not been impressive. Lawmakers, politicians, and news commentators make their greatest blunder leaving God out of the mix as they grapple with these social issues. This book offers the unique opportunity for a fresh look and new approach in dealing with these issues. The arguments presented within these pages are not only unique, but they are long overdue.

Corporate icons like Ford, Vanderbilt, Carnegie, Rockefeller, and J. P. Morgan understood that their corporations could not make a profit from production or from the salary given to the working class. They understood that profit is derived from consumption. Therefore, they gave their workers a large enough salary for them to purchase what they needed and wanted. In this way, workers benefitted from rising wages and corporations enjoyed rising profits. Needless to say, the economy boomed and consumption saw its best years. Within a few short years, this resulted in America defining itself and measuring its success by consumption. America became wedded to consumption in ways one could not imagine. To cap it off, the advertising industry blossomed and devoted itself to cultivating the passion for consumption.

Then, in the 1970s, things drastically changed. Corporate America came up with the brilliant idea to give the working class less money so that they would have more. Wages became minimal and were flattened. This meant that when there was a raise, it was just enough to keep the working class from becoming rich or independent. This resulted in the rich getting richer and the working class getting poorer.

Today, there is a vast gap between the incomes of the rich and the working class. "Between 1995 and 2004, the wealthiest 10 percent of American families saw their annual incomes rise about 40 percent, on average, from $216,000 to $302,000. In the same period, families in the middle 60 percent of the distribution scale saw their incomes rise just 20 percent, from an average of $39,000 in 1995 to an average of $46,000 in 2004. This has been especially disconcerting news."[1]

According to Austan Goolsbee, while productivity has risen during this same period of time, wages have been flattened, although many claim that an increase in productivity should result in an increase in wages. To further compound the matter, "these disparities in net worth have been growing even faster than the disparities in income. Since 1995, the top group has seen its average net worth grow 76 percent, from $1.8 million to $3.1 million, while those in the middle have seen their net worth grow about 36 percent, from $76,000 to $107,000. And that's before taxes. The after-tax numbers are even more dramatic, thanks to Bush administration policies that have sliced tax rates on high-income people, particularly on the income they derive from investments."[2]

These statistics contribute heavily to our discussion. These are not personal views to be debated in the court of public opinion; these figures are real. To ignore these figures is to flirt with economic disaster.

Within the midst of a failing economy, in 2008 the American people elected Barack Obama as president of the United States. This caught politicians on both side of the aisle completely off guard. President Obama emerged from the remote frontiers of obscurity and somehow managed to unseat the Clinton democratic dynasty and end the reign of white presidential supremacy in the White House.

Fiery in his rhetoric and a highly gifted orator, he mesmerized the masses both on the national and international stage. For billions he is not just another world leader. He is a link between a glorious past and a brighter future for America and the world. From the outset of his presidential campaign his motto and dictum has been monolithic—give the working class a piece of the pie and perhaps they will hang around for dinner. If the working class does better, everybody will do better.

Some feel that giving the working class a piece of the pie is similar to Robin Hood taking riches from the wealthy to give to the poor. But giving a piece of the pie to the working class is giving them what was always theirs—living wages! It means leveling the playing field and allowing them the same tax breaks given to the rich. If this were to be accomplished, the working class would be able to dream about the American Dream at night and get up and live it in the morning. This is a far cry from socialism. For the working class, President Obama is the embodiment of the new American Dream and the quintessence of the collective hopes and aspirations of the global proletariat. It appears that the American people are clamoring for a system that harnesses the best economic principles from both capitalism and socialism.

And yet, many people are scared away by the term "socialism." In his book *Liberal Fascism* Jonah Goldberg claims that the policies and principles on the liberal agenda are very similar to those of

---

1   Goolsbee, "Democratizing Capitalism," *Blueprint Magazine*.
2   Ibid.

Adolph Hitler. He states that both Hitler and Obama stole the hearts of the youth and awakened their interest in the political process. He goes further to align the two leaders, stating that they both were environmentalists, both publicly pushed the practice of good health habits, and both emphasized public education. Goldberg's postulation gets tricky and is blown out of proportion when he connects the dots and contends that modern progressivism and classical fascism share common intellectual roots.[3]

The broth from this soup is too thin to nourish such a robust rationale. Didn't Esau and Jacob share a common womb from Rebecca? Yet it is written, "Jacob have I loved, but Esau have I hated" (Rom. 9:13, KJV). Let's look at another comparison. Dr. Martin Luther King Jr. adapted Mahatma Gandhi's philosophy of non-violence in the civil rights movement. Who would conclude that the civil rights movement of the United States of America and Gandhi's struggle for independence from British oppression is one and the same?

Just because Obama shares some ideologies that are similar to those of Hitler does not mean his administration is comparable with that of the Third Reich. Nazi Germany is Nazi Germany, and the United States of America is the United States of America—the twain shall never be same. Take for example this analogy: If a vulture is placed in a cage, its first instinct is to scour every crick and corner for carrion. Put an eagle in that same cage, and, with an air of regality, it will fix its eyes on the sun. It is the same cage, but it is a different bird. The point is that people should be judged by who they are and not by what they are perceived to be.

Assertions of fascism may sound strange to American ears, but fascism is seen every day in a free enterprise society in which the poor are systematically looted, plundered, pillaged, and exploited by corporate opportunists. All this is done with the consenting approval of the government. This has led many to conclude that fascism occurs when corporations shape government policies and engage in lobbying. Many citizens in the global community still reject the socialism that is defined as being of the government, by the government, and for the government. In this economic system, riches are taken from the rich and distributed to the poor. Instead of buying into this traditional definition of socialism, more and more individuals are gravitating toward the mindset of a moderate version of socialism in which the state levels the playing field for equal opportunities; creates safety nets for those hit the hardest by misfortune, old age, and sickness; and protects citizens from the abuses of Wall Street.

According to Bruce Norman, the heartbeat of postmodernism is making a difference in people's lives. Community is of utmost importance to the millennial generation. Sectarianism, capitalism, socialism, totalitarianism, imperialism, communism, denominationalism, etc. pale in comparison to loving God supremely and loving our neighbors as ourselves.[4]

People don't care how much you know, what position you hold, how much power you have, how much truth you have, and what denomination you belong to. They want to know how much you care.[5]

---

3   Goldberg, *Liberal Fascism: The Secret History of the American Left, from Mussolini to the Politics of Change*, pp. 19, 166, 167, 391.
4   Norman, *Bridging the Gap: Reaching the Internet Generation: An Evangelistic Strategy for Reaching the Postmodern Generation*, p. 25.
5   Maxwell, *Developing the Leader Within You*, pp. 6, 7.

Even though both socialism and capitalism fall short on expectations, it is undisputed that both reflect to some degree the pure pretenses of some godly principles. Mother Teresa rightly earned the respect of postmodernism when she wrote, "By blood, I am Albanian. By citizenship, an Indian. By faith, I am a Catholic nun. As to my calling, I belong to the world. As to my heart, I belong entirely to the Heart of Jesus."[6] She acted on her words by caring for one of the most ostracized groups in modern society—contagious lepers.

In the postmodern niche, the fatherhood of God, our Creator, and the brotherhood of humanity are paramount. The fabric of humanity is woven with different stories, but all hold common hopes. We may be from different countries of origin, but there is a universal desire to move forward in a common direction, and love is the unique international "glue" that can hold us together. The common denominators underscored along the great continuum of human life suggest that everyone is equally, albeit diversely, suited. The human consensus is "not only to recognize the common humanity of all in all our particularities but also to work together with one another to produce those social [socioreligious] conditions without which we cannot be human and which we can only create together, not separately.... No one is indeed free unless all are free."[7]

Our destinies are tied up in each other's destinies. Martin Luther King Jr. penned it rather succinctly when he wrote that "all men are caught in an inescapable network of mutuality."[8] Cross Daman wrote in Richard Wright's *Outsider*, "I wish I had some way to make a bridge from man to man.... [Beside God] Man is all we've got."[9]

The rationale of the postmodern creed is that if you help others reach the top of the mountain, you will be closer to the top yourself. The essence of this book can be summed up in the following statement: Smart corporations make sure the working class is making a living wage; the corporation in turn receives that which they want, increased production, consumption, and solid profits. This argument is overpowering and virtually unstoppable when considered within the context of "loving God supremely and loving your neighbor as yourself," which is the common creed shared by three of the greatest religions of the world—Judaism, Islam, and Christianity. Postmodernism in its purest sense is a stubborn reminder "that every man is an heir of the legacy of dignity and worth."[10]

---

6   Mother Teresa, "Mother Teresa of Calcutta (1910–1997)," The Holy See, http://1ref.us/n.
7   Kyongsuk, *The Solidarity of Others in a Divided World: A Postmodern Theology After Postmodernism*, p. 137.
8   King, "Quotation #32615 from Classic Quotes," The Quotations Page, http://1ref.us/o.
9   Bolton, *People's Skills: How to Assert Yourself, Listen to others, and Resolve Conflicts*, p. 3.
10 King, *A Knock at Midnight: Inspiration from the Great Sermons of Reverend Martin Luther King, Jr.*, pp. 86, 87.

Chapter 2

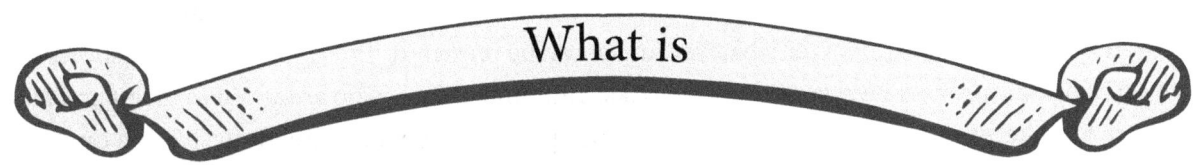

What is Capitalism?

Overview

When compared to its historical counterparts, the economic performance of capitalism is off the charts. It has produced widespread prosperity at a level previously unknown. Competing economic systems, including communism, have been eating its dust for years as this economic juggernaut gallops at record-breaking speed to its rendezvous with success and global economic dominance. Having disparaged every other contender, capitalism sits alone in the driver's seat. Notwithstanding, something is drastically wrong with this economic system. It has an Achilles heel called unrestrained human nature.

Defining Capitalism

Capitalism or free enterprise is hard to categorize or define. Robert Tracinski, editor of the Intellectual Activist, describes capitalism as "the only moral social system because it is the only system that respects the freedom of the producers to think and the right of the individual to set his own goals and pursue his [her] own happiness."[1] Where I disagree with his definition is in the statement that individuals are able to set their own goals and pursue their own happiness. For the majority of the working class, corporate bosses determine their goals and their degree of happiness. What kind of goals or degree of happiness can an individual pursue who is working a minimum-wage job that pays an average of $15,000 annually?

The swiftness with which capitalism took the driver's seat as the world's most accepted and admired economy is breathtaking and begs the question as to its origin and its future.[2] "Capitalism is the

---

[1] Tracinski, "The Moral Basis of Capitalism," The Center for the Advancement of Capitalism, The Center for the Advancement of Capitalism, http://1ref.us/p.
[2] Welch, "Everymoney: Capitalism, Democracy and Global Wealth: Part 1," *Vision*, http://1ref.us/q.

only system that fully allows and encourages the virtues necessary for human life. It is the only system that safeguards the freedom of the independent mind and recognizes the sanctity of the individual."[3]

Because it operates within the friendly confines of a free society, competition is the heartbeat of capitalism. In this system, all property is privately or corporately owned. Investments are the engine that drives capitalism. Therefore, individuals have to continually exert themselves to unharness the most advantageous employment for whatever capital can be mustered. Those who want to be successful in a capitalist setting must be prepared to take risks. Thus, individuals who are afraid to invest and take risks are less likely to succeed in the world of free enterprise. If individuals are to survive in a capitalist economy, they must sever all sentimental ties with society and focus on the main objective—making a profit!

Capitalism is more concerned about who has what rather than who gets what. "It is almost color blind, the only hue that it ultimately cares about being the tint of currencies and coins."[4] Capitalism rewards greed, which is why at times it supports the democratic position and in other instances supports the republican agenda. It all depends which agenda is more financially beneficial. For instance, modern capitalism is reluctant to do away the three main welfare subsidies—Temporary Assistance for Needy Families, Supplemental Nutrition Assistance Program, and Supplemental Security Income—because this system provides an unending supply of poor workers who are forced to work for a pittance, while the corporations rake in huge profits.

What is capitalism? According to William Welch, it is a socioeconomic system that is still young within the scope of the global marketplace. It boasts of an ascendancy of only 500 years. Nevertheless, "it has grown to occupy a dominant position in the global social economy and has become the de facto model for business, finance and government economic policy."[5] The leading economic giants, the likes of Adam Smith, Robert Malthus, David Ricardo, Karl Marx, John Maynard Keynes and Joseph Schumpeter, all walked across the economical stage of capitalism. They played their parts exceedingly well. Their diplomacies, ideas, suggestions, and input have reformed and refined capitalism over recent centuries.[6]

Capitalism has mushroomed into a global hegemonic powerhouse, leaving her subsumed weaker "siblings" in consternation and bemused indifference. "Since the end of World War II, its economic performance is off the charts when compared to its historical counterparts, producing widespread prosperity at a level previously unknown."[7] Capitalism has harnessed global signatories. Competing economic systems, including communism, have been eating its dust as this economic juggernaut gallops at record-breaking speed to its rendezvous with success and global mastery. Capitalism "might simply be viewed as a sound economic system whereby each of us reaps the benefit of our own labor.

---

3   Tracinski, "The Moral Basis of Capitalism," The Center for the Advancement of Capitalism, http://1ref.us/p.
4   Larson, "Capitalism: What Were Its Moral Strengths and Weaknesses? Part 1," *Spectrum,* http://1ref.us/r..
5   Welch, "Everymoney: Capitalism, Democracy and Global Wealth: Part 1," *Vision,* http://1ref.us/q.
6   Ibid.
7   Ibid.

Under a capitalist system, someone who is willing to work hard and do a job well will likely prosper more than someone who is lazy or who takes shortcuts."[8]

It will be shown in the subsequent chapters why this philosophy does not always hold true. Workers who are downsized to satiate the political thirst of greed could hardly be categorized as lazy or taking shortcuts. Capitalism was birthed in an economic system in which self-interest is a difficult conundrum. It would quickly take a spiraling dive and crumble like a house made of cards if deprived of the freedom to exercise such a problematic idiosyncrasy. The freedom that a rich man needs to maintain and add to his wealth is the same freedom a poor man needs to create his wealth. "A system that sacrifices the self to 'society' is a system of slavery—and a system that sacrifices thinking to coercion is a system of brutality."[9] Democracy provides such freedom and liberty.

The Achilles Heel of Capitalism

It is obvious that something is drastically wrong with free enterprise. There is nothing wrong with the ideal of capitalism, which in essence states that people who work hard will be successful and will have the funds they need to take care of themselves and their families. The major problem is "the way *people* operate within the system."[10] Every individual has the freedom to become an entrepreneur, but the system becomes tainted with immorality and inhumaneness when corporations refuse to give workers proper benefits, such as health care coverage, giving them the least so that they can pocket hefty profits. Modern capitalism is guilty of purposefully keeping minorities on welfare to perpetuate poverty and dependence so that there are enough workers for minimum-wage jobs. In the end, this results in higher profits for the employers until their coffers are overflowing.

An economic system that looks the other way when billions of dollars of taxpayers' money bails out banks and corporations who misused the funds, but condemns raising minimum wage to a living wage because it is taking away from the rich to give to the poor, has become a danger to itself. So what name is given to an economic system in which money is taken away from the poor and given to the rich? Modern capitalism has gone beyond hard work and taking risks. This system has evolved into a harbinger for greed, skullduggery, and exploitation of the working class.

"In other words, it is unrestrained human nature that forms the Achilles heel of the system."[11] It is the dark side of the human soul that is its most prominent nemesis. Capitalism parades the personalization of national interest as a façade for the nationalization of personal interest.

Capitalism is a nauseating socioeconomic system. "Countless hundreds of millions of people have died in the last 100 years because of capitalism's wars, and from the poverty, starvation, and preventable disease capitalism produces. The toll of human life and misery and ecological destruction have had the sole purpose of keeping a tiny minority of the population in power, wealth and privilege."[12]

---

8 Ibid.
9 Tracinski, "The Moral Basis of Capitalism," The Center for the Advancement of Capitalism, http://1ref.us/p.
10 Meakin, "The Achilles' Heel of Capitalism," *Vision*, http://1ref.us/s.
11 Ibid.
12 "A Friend of the Capitalists," *Thr@ll*, http://1ref.us/t.

Perhaps capitalism's greatest display of hypocrisy is that it condemns socializing wealth as socialism, but socializing poverty gets a free ride.[13] This is evident in the federal stimulus package to bail out U.S. corporations, which was met with little or no resistance. On the other hand, in a time when unemployment rates were through the roof, in the early hours of the new year of 2014, the proposed extension of the unemployment benefit fund was shot down by Congress.

However, there is yet another bend along the capitalistic highway of economic success. Free enterprise can only thrive in freedom. This opens the door for "competition with other self-interested people, particularly where interests coincide or overlap."[14] In order for companies to become financially successful, they are forced to "compete for business, market share, geographic or sector dominance."[15]

In this economic system, "entrepreneurs pay producers as little as possible and charge consumers as much as they can. Over time, the rich get richer and the poor get poorer. Eventually, neither can afford to buy or sell and the economy 'crashes and burns'"[16] and weaker corporations close down. These twists and turns illustrate the opportunistic nature of the corporate world.

For the capitalist, this is a blessing in disguise. "Like forest fires that consume the dead and weak [in the ecological system], recessions and depressions eliminate sick businesses that should have disappeared much earlier."[17] Stronger enterprises emerge to reshape the economic landscape. A heavy casualty is that these economic downturns also burn people.

One of the most pathetic signatures of capitalism is that it treats the working class as depreciated machinery, not as human beings. Its pretenses are diametrically opposed to Adam Smith's position that consumers are the most important link in the chain of wealth formation. The hallmark of its misery is that the capitalist elite swim in the very sea of wealth that drowns the working class. In a February 2011 address to the Chamber of Commerce, U.S. President Barack Obama reported that "American companies have nearly $2 trillion sitting on their balance sheet."[18]

Capitalism's foremost misdemeanor is that bribery and favoritism, not merit, are often the paths frequently traveled to promotions and appointments. It has been rightly argued that there is nothing inherently wrong with self-interest. The problem is that too often such self-interest heads in the direction of "looking after our own interests *at the expense* of our neighbor's."[19]

The Two Classes in Capitalism

Two diametrically opposed main classes define free enterprise—the capitalist and the working class. It may be popular to talk about other societal "classes" such as the "upper," "middle," and "lower or poor" class, but it really boils down to the capitalists and the working class. Notwithstanding, it is this

---

13 Welch, "Everymoney: Capitalism, Democracy and Global Wealth: Part 2," *Vision,* http://1ref.us/u.
14 Meakin, "The Achilles' Heel of Capitalism," *Vision,* http://1ref.us/s.
15 Ibid.
16 Larson, "Capitalism: What Were Its Moral Strengths and Weaknesses? Part 1," *Spectrum,* http://1ref.us/r.
17 Ibid.
18 "America's Paradox: Broke Government, Rich Corporations," Business Insider, http://1ref.us/v.
19 Meakin, "The Achilles' Heel of Capitalism," *Vision,* http://1ref.us/s.

division that is the key in understanding what free enterprise is all about. Under this system, a small minority of people own the land, factories, technology sector, transport system, etc. They also have the means for producing and distributing goods. We refer to this group of people as the capitalist class.[20]

In a book review of Paul Kivel's work *You Call This a Democracy? Who Benefits, Who Pays and Who Really Decides?*, the reviewer wrote that the book "explains what the ruling class is (those with a family income above $373,000 and net financial wealth of at least $2 million), how it controls the government, media, and economy, and the negative effects we all suffer."[21]

Many believe that the "ruling class" is behind every significant political and economic decision made in the United States of America. Sadly, the capitalist class represents only 2 percent of the entire United States population. They wield an influence on the economy and society far beyond their numbers. Often disguised as "special interest groups," they strive to perpetuate their agenda by passing on assets, lifestyles, values, and social networks from one generation to the next.

They lead the charge in investment decisions, which ultimately impact millions of people in the working class. They contribute special interest money to political parties that support their agenda. Their fingerprints are all over the media and modern technology. It is not beyond their reach to sabotage websites and manipulate polls in order to influence the thinking of other classes. Democracy is not up for sale in America. It has been bought, sold, and paid for by the capitalist class.[22] This was why Tony Benn wrote, "Democracy is always a struggle for justice against the powerful."[23] America starts wars to democratize other nations, but it feels as if there is no true democracy in the land of the free and the home of the brave.

In the Gettysburg Address, Abraham Lincoln said that a "government of the people, by the people, for the people, shall not perish from the earth."[24] However, America is no longer governed by the people. Neither is it run by the congressional, judiciary, or executive branches of government. It appears that America is a government of the special interest group, by the special interest group, and for the special interest group.

An example of how the capitalist class and special interest groups operate is seen in the Affordable Care Act passed by Congress and upheld by the United States Supreme Court. The working class stands to benefit the most from health care reform. However, special interest groups lobbied against the law because corporations will be obligated to provide full health coverage to all their workers, which will cost the corporations more. The same battle is fought over minimum wage. Most Americans support raising the minimum wage, yet special interest groups condemn this move as a subtle version of socialism.

---

20 "What Is Capitalism?" World Socialist Movement, http://1ref.us/w.
21 Knight, "Review of 'You Call This a Democracy? Who Benefits, Who Pays, and Who Really Decides?" End of Capitalism, http://1ref.us/x.
22 Gottschalk, "A U.S. View: Democracy, Bought and Paid For," Rabble.ca, http://1ref.us/y.
23 "Tony Benn Biography," Biography Online, http://1ref.us/z.
24 "The Gettysburg Address," Abraham Lincoln Online, http://1ref.us/10.

The capitalistic system rives employers to painstakingly calculate their employees' salaries to ensure that the working class never becomes rich. If they did become rich, the thought is that they would no longer need to work.[25] Capitalism cannot survive without poverty. By definition, its name suggests that it "capitalizes" on the misfortunes of those from the lower reaches of society. In every epoch of American history, the capitalist class has held themselves superior to the working class. Inequality has always epitomized the American society. It was capitalism that institutionalized it.

The capitalist class operates on the principle that the working class is paid to produce goods and services that are sold for a profit. Capitalist corporations are keenly aware that the tendering of concessions is a highly lucrative industry. Therefore, cheap labor is capitalism's best friend. "The capitalists live off the profits they obtain from exploiting the working class whilst reinvesting some of their profits for the further accumulation of wealth."[26]

The system is able to buttress its credentials by convincing the populace that they live in the best country in the world. In the meantime, the genuine suffering of the poor has been diluted in the strong solution of a dominant United States culture. Politicians and other capitalists peddle the idea to the world that the only poor in America are those who are lazy. "Pull up your boot straps" they say to an individual who has neither boots nor straps. The capitalist class continues to frown upon the growing numbers from the working classes who are knocking incessantly at its gates in a desperate attempt to improve their socioeconomic conditions.

Divide and Conquer

No government or corporation can control a populace that is united and free from segregation, inequality, and exploitation. Because of this, class division is an essential feature of capitalism. Societal classes are free enterprise's masterpiece invention to perpetuate its economic empire. Therefore, in capitalism, it is imperative that social forces, based on real or imaginary differences, remain centrifugal. This is done by creating divisions that cut across society. This book contends that it is the class division and the drive to make profit that is the root of most of the world's current problems. This ranges from starvation, war, crime, and alienation. One ethnicity gets the "carrots," and the other is given the "stick." A certain segment of the population is pulled up from the degradations of welfare by offering them jobs with living wages. On the other hand, another group from the same population is purposefully kept on welfare and is paid a low wage. One group is compelled by law to sit at the back seats of public transport, while another group is allowed to sit at the front. Educate one group, while the other group is kept ignorant. Class division is tailor-made for capitalism.

Profit or Need Satisfaction?

"Every aspect of our lives is subordinated to the worst excesses of the drive to make profit. In capitalist society, our real needs will only ever come a poor second to the requirements of profit."[27]

---

25 "What Is Capitalism?" World Socialist Movement, http://1ref.us/w.
26 Ibid.
27 Ibid.

Capitalism is based on selling a product for a profit, but in order for a company to sell a good, it needs human labor and materials. "For example, a bottled water might be produced by taking water from a spring in Maine and putting a plastic bottle and label around it. The bottle in turn was produced from oil pumped in Saudi Arabia, chemically altered in Louisiana and given shape in China. The bottle is shipped to a store for you to spend $1 on water (which used to be free). Each of these steps creates pollution and waste, much of which would never biodegrade. Likewise, every step of the process, from the factory workers to the oil workers to the truck drivers and the supermarket clerks, but none of them feels any connection to the final product or to you, the consumer. It is probably fair to say they would be doing other things if they didn't need the money. They work dull jobs because they have to. Of your $1, perhaps 10 cents is divided between them [the workers]. Some money goes into manufacturing, shipping, packaging, and management costs. The majority likely goes towards advertising and profit. Much of the profit will be reinvested to produce more bottles of water so that the company can attain a greater share of the beverage market."[28]

The quest for profits is the impetus that drives free enterprise. Always ready to sell it services to the highest bidder, capitalism is driven by making the most money possible, regardless of who gets "stepped on" as capitalists clamor to reach the top of the ladder. If the entire economic structure stands on the shaky foundation of greed, then profit must be the chief cornerstone. For example, it goes undisputed that in industrialized cities like Los Angeles, greenhouse gas masks are needed more than name brand sports equipment. But nobody walks around with greenhouse gas masks. Instead, the entire city is crawling with name brand sports equipment. The capitalist mentality drives corporations to produce and sell products that people need and don't need. You see, the decisive factor in the capitalist world is not consumer satisfaction or need, it is what capitalists determine can be sold at a profit.

In the marketplace of the free world, capitalistic greed and selfishness are king. This is why corporate America came up with ways to keep the public consuming products they don't need. The advertising industry, wedded to special holidays and sale days, was born. However, it is unfair to blame individual capitalists for capitalistic greed. The truth is that "they do not have a choice about it. The need to make a profit is imposed on capitalists as a condition for not losing their investments and their position … Competition with other capitalists forces them to reinvest as much of their profits as they can afford to keep their means and methods of production up to date."[29]

In capitalism, dominance and the elimination of potential challengers is the key to success. Putting it in simple terms, the Golden Rule in capitalism is that the person who has the gold rules. The wealthy hold disproportionate power within the establishment, which allows them to preserve their interests and make more money. It is for this reason that Michel Beaud wrote in his book *A History of Capitalism, 1500–2000* that "in each epoch, capitalism has been both creative and destructive, but today it is the very existence of humanity and the planet which is at stake."[30]

---

28 Knight, "Part 2. What is Capitalism?" End of Capitalism, http://1ref.us/11.
29 "What Is Capitalism?" World Socialist Movement, http://1ref.us/w.
30 Welch, "Everymoney: Capitalism, Democracy and Global Wealth: Part 3," *Vision*, http://1ref.us/12.

Divorced from human fanaticisms, excesses, class division, and greed, capitalism would be a power for good to contend with. This was the capitalism Adam Smith had in mind in the eighteenth century when he set afoot the American Revolution in economics. It was a democratized capitalism in which independent producers had the control of exchanging their goods for mutual benefits. Unfortunately, modern capitalism is a monopoly controlled by the rich elite.

The closest example of a bona fide democratized economic system may be the *kibbutz* system still practiced in certain places in Israel. In such a system, independent producers exchange goods for their mutual benefits. "The *kibbutz* (Hebrew word for 'communal settlement') is a unique rural community; a society dedicated to mutual aid and social justice; a socioeconomic system based on the principle of joint ownership of property, equality and cooperation of production, consumption and education; the fulfillment of the idea 'from each according to his ability, to each according to his needs'; a home for those who have chosen it."[31]

---

31 "The Kibbutz," Jewish Virtual Library, http://1ref.us/13.

Chapter 3

A Brief History of Capitalism?

Overview

Studying capitalism and its past facilitates the negotiation of its future, making it clearer and more predictable. It is from this vantage that a viable solution for the recovery of a broken economy is suggested. This chapter highlights how Adam Smith and the American Revolution contributed to the birth of capitalism. In studying the history of capitalism, we will also examine the American culture and how capitalism was exported to the third world from the "living room" of the American television industry.

Before Capitalism

A pure form of capitalism has never existed; however, America came the closest of any country in embracing its ideals in the nineteenth century. Postmodern America is a far cry from being a pure capitalist country. Instead, the country is a "mixed economy" of freedom and control that is diluted by the monopoly of the special interest groups. As we look at history, we discover that capitalism was brought about by revolution. We play a dangerous game when the past is snubbed and despised, giving the nod to the distinctive indulgences of the millennial era. Past success in a given economy is indispensable and conducive for the upward mobility of its contemporary performance.

Paul Johnson was on target when he penned that "history is a powerful antidote to contemporary arrogance."[1] Maya Angelou had it right when she wrote, "History, despite its wrenching pain, cannot be unlived, but if faced with courage, need not be lived again."[2] Our view of history shapes how we live in the present and, therefore, dictates what answers we offer for our current economic problems. Notwithstanding, there is a bend in the road to economic success. Past successes or failures should not

---

1 Johnson, *The Quotable Paul Johnson: A Topical Compilation of His Wit, Wisdom and Satire*, p. 138
2 Angelou, Brainy Quote, http://1ref.us/14.

be allowed to dictate the path the United States economy should travel today. Different times demand fresh approaches and a new line of attack. Navigating the treacherous currents of an economic downturn takes a spiraling divisive dive when past economical glories are manipulated to belittle and stifle the innovative efforts of modern economists. "What would Reagan do?" pales in comparison to what should be done.

Land Capital

There are evidences that free enterprise, as we know it today, arose from plantations and small rural communities. This system was very distinct from modern capitalism, which was planted and took root during the Industrial Revolution. During the early sixteenth century, land was the principal form of capital. It was controlled by royalty, the aristocracy, or the Catholic Church. Until King Henry VIII confiscated its monasteries, the Catholic Church owned a quarter of English soil. "Wealth, not surprisingly, was often defined in terms of land use, primarily agriculture."[3]

"Up until the 12th century, less than 5% of the population of Europe lived in towns. Skilled workers lived in the city but received their keep from feudal lords rather than a real wage, and the farmers were essentially serfs for landed nobles."[4] The working class worked hard. The good thing was that they didn't have to sell their labor to any capitalist boss who would manipulate the wages to gain hefty profits. Instead, they were forced to exchange crops, giving some to landlords for rent and some to the government as tax. They subsisted on what was left. At this junction, defined borders, armies, and unified markets were nowhere in sight.[5] "However, as 20th-century economist Robert L. Heilbroner pointed out in *The Worldly Philosophers,* 'although land was salable under certain conditions (with many strings attached) it was not generally for sale.' "[6] Notwithstanding, there were times when land in some respects was salable. This was not so when it came to labor. "Serfs, apprentices, and journeymen had only limited rights, and work was highly structured and controlled."[7]

The Bourgeoisie Revolutions

Haunted by waning fortunes, peasant laborers were unable to acquire land. Therefore, they were powerless to make independent decisions that would produce wealth. In this aspect, there have not been many amendments reflected in modern capitalism. The working class is still denied enough capital to do some small time investing. This social barricade is why the "precapitalistic society did not embrace the concept of making a living. Work was not a means to an end but an end in itself. For the working masses, economic and social life were one and the same."[8]

---

3   Welch, "Everymoney: Capitalism, Democracy and Global Wealth: Part 1," *Vision*, http://1ref.us/q.
4   Beattie, "The History of Capitalism: From Feudalism to Wall Street," Investopedia, http://1ref.us/15.
5   Ibid.
6   Welch, "Everymoney: Capitalism, Democracy and Global Wealth: Part 1," *Vision*, http://1ref.us/q.
7   Ibid.
8   Ibid.

"By the 18th century, wealth was still controlled by the privileged few. One thing was clearly changing, however: capital was no longer restricted to the ownership of land."[9] The time of the bourgeoisie revolution had come. The bourgeoisie were considered to be the middle class. They owned capital and were held in regard because of their job, education, or wealth. This was in contrast to their counterparts who had money and land because they were born into a family of prominence.

"To be a king then implied the exercise of real power rather than the duties of a highly esteemed public servant; to be a member of the aristocracy implied the ownership of land and a position of privilege in the community; and membership of the bourgeoisie, that class of—people who controlled capital, factories, labour and other means of production, marked the first steps towards social importance."[10]

"In England and France, peasants and independent craft workers participated in mass movements, led by the more determined bourgeois elements, that overthrew the existing state to the benefit of the bourgeoisie. These movements were held together by radical politics such as that of the Jacobins in France."[11] These revolutions were political transformations from the middle and created the conditions for capitalism.

The "bourgeois revolutions" flourished as they reconstituted themselves into a small clandestine movement that created a system of local competition, wage labor, and nation states. These revolutions were thorough and comprehensive. The competitions were limited to the proletariat and not the corporations. This is in opposition to the norm in modern capitalism. It is of noticeable importance that the bourgeois revolutions started as an uprising from the middle up. This was out of step with what was the rule for many of the world's most powerful states, in which revolutions were generated from above. Seizing the moment, they created unified national markets and did away with the remaining setbacks. This unknowingly paved the way for capitalism.

"Once bourgeois revolutions had created the conditions for capitalism in England and France, the ruling classes of other states had to adapt in order to compete."[12] The ruling class did this out of fear of the threat posed to their interests by the working class emerging under capitalism. In an ironic twist of history, by 1871 a prominent landowner with grandiose ambitions named Otto von Bismarck singlehandedly "headed a unified German state that had defeated France in war and became the most important capitalist power in Europe."[13] Capitalism was conceived in the womb of the emerging working class.

Mercantilism and Hegemony

From the 1500s to the 1700s, gold and trade were the acid test of a good or bad economy.[14] This mentality provoked inevitable economic changes. A mercantile milieu was born, and the entire

---
9   Ibid.
10 McBratney, "The Rise of the Bourgeoisie," Lisburn.com, http://1ref.us/16.
11 Allinson, "How Did Capitalism Come Into Being?" Socialist Worker, http://1ref.us/17.
12 Ibid.
13 Ibid.
14 Welch, "Everymoney: Capitalism, Democracy and Global Wealth: Part 1," *Vision*, http://1ref.us/q.

world became amenable to trade and commerce. This was a natural outgrowth as each nation tried to strengthen its economic position in the growing world, for mercantilism is the development of nationalistic economic policies. During this epoch, precious metals, from which money was coined, were esteemed as the greatest asset one could have. The temperature of gold fever ran high, and special effort was made to obtain the largest possible quantities of gold. The tombs of ancient kings were plundered in order to assuage the gold fever. The countries that could not obtain precious metals from the New World had to resort to trading of luxury goods, precious stones, ivory, silk porcelain, furs, skins, spices, aromatics, slaves, and wild animals. The goal was to sell as much merchandise as possible and buy less.

"Because of this, nations kept wages low and encouraged population growth to ensure their continued ability to produce sufficient exports at low prices. [Like modern capitalism,] the resulting benefits and prosperity, however, did not flow down to the average citizen, who remained poor and overworked."[15] Nothing has changed to this day. Politicians are still insisting on the failed policies of trickle down "Reaganomics."

A dramatic shift in the economic landscape unfolded. The concept of wealth and power shifted away from land to trade. This paved the way for banking and the emergence of a merchant class between the upper, middle, and working classes. This represented a significant advance in the direction of an emerging capitalistic society. Thus, "the way was opened to the idea that the wealth of the kingdom depended on the wealth of the merchants and manufacturers."[16] Let the truth be told, the wealth of a nation rides on the shoulders of consumption, not on those of the manufacturers. Africa, India, and the New World were probably the most lucrative branches of foreign trade for centuries.

Merchants were able to exchange very cheap products for gold. Capital returns from the shipping trade were astronomical and optimum. According to Efrain Karsh, the Jews played a central role in this European trading industry. They traded in agriculture for commercialism, and because they were a people group who spoke other languages, it positioned them between the greedy potentates and fanatic mobs of other countries.[17] Trade prospered until marauders and pillagers increasingly harassed trade routes and violence became endemic, causing merchants and financiers to become wary of the risks involved.

"Confronted with this dilemma, the ever resourceful merchants and financiers invented … the "joint-stock" company, predecessor of the modern corporation…. This important innovation provided two essential elements that would foster capitalism's development: the sharing of risk, and limitations on personal liabilities. Now merchants could pool their money and share the risk of long-distance ocean trade, thereby limiting their personal liability."[18]

They could do so using someone else's money to fund these joint ventures and pay them back from the generous returns. Not to mention the heavy profit they would make. Borrowing, which is

---

15 Ibid.
16 Ibid., quoted from Michel Beaud's *A History of Capitalism, 1500–2000*.
17 Karsh, *Islamic Imperialism: A History*, p. 69.
18 Welch, "Everymoney: Capitalism, Democracy and Global Wealth: Part 1," *Vision*, http://1ref.us/q.

indispensable to capitalism, allowed "merchants to assume risks and enter business deals that they could or chose not to enter into using solely their own capital. At around this same time, investors also concluded that simply being able to invest and withdraw capital in a joint-stock company wasn't good enough. Why not trade or negotiate one's interest on an open exchange?"[19] This concept became a reality when the Amsterdam Stock Exchange was established in 1602, becoming the forerunner of the stock exchange.

Fetus of Capitalism

The components of the "fetus" of capitalism were taking shape as early as the 1500s. "Merchant commerce, banking, the joint-stock company structure and the stock exchange laid the key foundations." However, a revolution was the final component necessary to cause the "birth" of capitalism. "A revolution in economic thought and … in politics … [converged] in the latter part of the 18th century. Adam Smith would publish *An Inquiry into the Nature and Causes of the Wealth of Nation,* and the American colonies would declare themselves independent of Great Britain, both in 1776."[20]

Capitalism now had a means to travel first class in the vehicle of democracy under the pledge of "life, liberty, and the pursuit of happiness for all." Smith "viewed wealth as the sum of the goods *consumed* by *all* people in society.… [This radical position was at variance with the accepted norm of that time.] Prior to this, the ownership of capital and the benefits of the economy were restricted to the privileged elite. Smith recognized, for the first time, the importance of the consumer (each individual in society) in the formation of wealth."[21]

A healthy economy is maintained on the footing of prosperity for both the working and capitalist classes. It is only from this vantage point that economic sailing will be smooth and equitable.

Adam Smith's The Theory of Moral Sentiments

With all his prodigious skills and insights, Adam Smith, the author of *The Theory of Moral Sentiments*, was a quintessential economist. He was the undisputed embodiment of capitalism of the eighteenth century and the forerunner of modern capitalism. According to Smith, the greatest ruffian and the hardened violator of society are born with a moral sense. Our conscience, which is innate, tells us what is right and wrong. This is not something bequeathed to us by lawmakers or by rational analysis. Smith states that human beings are born with an inherent concern for the fortunes and misfortunes of others. Therefore, people, with absolutely no input from the government, will be able to live together in an orderly and beneficial manner because of a feeling that humans possess called "sympathy." He hypothesizes that this also holds true for mankind's economic actions.

The Theory of Moral Sentiments advocates for a new liberalism in which social organization is seen as the final precipitate of human input. It is proposed that our sense of conscience and sympathy

---

19 Ibid.
20 Ibid.
21 Ibid.

enables us to live together in orderly and beneficial social organizations. In this way, our morality is the product of our nature and not our reason. Using the illustration of the butcher, Smith goes to bat for corporations. People get their food from the butcher, but the butcher has his own interest in mind as he is trying to sell you your dinner.[22] Therefore, it is a waste of precious time for the working class to appeal to the humanitarian side of corporate bosses; instead, they should appeal to their self-love.

Corporations turn a profit when the working class consumes the products they produce. Within these perimeters, corporations understand that if the working class is given living wages they will have more money to spend on products and the economy will grow. However, there is a different perspective today. Some view the raising of minimum wages to living wages as a subtle version of socialism, which they feel will slow down the economy. They contend that increasing the price of employment will result in less production and less sales. There are others who take an oppositional stance to this position, contending that raising the minimum wage is not increasing the price of employment but is simply paying workers what they should be paid. Therefore, they state that raising the minimum wage will save the economy.

Smith's theories summon both the capitalist and working classes to an intensified interaction and honest dialogue around humanity's table of brotherhood. Both classes must have the common sense to forge out an idyllic coexistence or they are doomed to perish together as fools. Unfortunately, the importance of production, and in particular consumption, has been diluted in a strong solution of greed and skullduggery. This is why economies crash and burn.

"Smith found in the mechanism of the market a self-regulating system for society's orderly provisioning."[23] For him, the individual lies at the heart of capitalism. Economic prosperity in capitalism is guaranteed to the individual who eliminates the middleman. When constructing a building, the bulk of the work is handled by the sub-contractors. The contractor may or may not hold a hammer in his or her hand. Eliminating the middleman, in this case the contractor, would save the owners tons of money. Corporations the likes of Walmart have eliminated the middleman and are reaping a harvest of economic success.

The Missing Ingredient

Implicit in Smith's theory, however, is a telling omission. The failure to acknowledge that there is a dark side of the human soul. "The heart [i.e., the human mind] is deceitful above all things and beyond cure. Who can understand it?" (Jer. 17:9, NIV). Capitalism has an Achilles heel called unrestrained human nature. It can become problematic if left to function alone on its own devices. Some peddle the idea that human nature is deceitful when it operates in a socialist setting. "The constituency will lay back and take advantage of the system" is the cry. On the other hand, that very same deceitful human nature somehow mysteriously becomes sanctified under a capitalistic regime that privatizes wealth. In other words, the "engine" of Smith's theory kicks into high gear when driving along the "highway" of

---

22   Ibid.
23   Ibid.

a capitalist setting but stalls on the "expressway" of socialism? I beg to differ! The deceitfulness of the human heart wreaks havoc in both systems.

The Betrayal of Adam Smith

Corporate capitalists tried to maneuver themselves into the driver's seat of the global economy by crying "socialism" at every noble effort to give a piece of the pie to the working class. Capitalism, as it parades itself today, is a flagrant violation of most of what Smith stood for. He was betrayed by the peddled mendacity that he was opposed to any form of governmental regulation. However, in all fairness, during his lifetime most governments were monarchies. The possibility of governmental regulation perhaps never occurred to him. "Corporate [capitalists] libertarians maintain that the market turns unrestrained greed into socially optimal outcomes. Smith would be outraged by those who attribute this idea to him. He was talking about [seventeenth-century] small farmers and artisans trying to get the best price for their products to provide for themselves and their families. This is self-interest, not greed."[24] It is ironic that some people feel that Smith hated government and loved corporations—he strongly disliked both. "He viewed government primarily as an instrument for extracting taxes to subsidize elites and intervening in the market to protect corporate monopolies. In his words, 'Civil government, so far as it is instituted for the security of property, is in reality instituted for the defense of the rich against the poor, or of those who have some property against those who have none at all.'"[25]

Nothing has changed to this day. The more things change, the more they remain the same. By his own confession, it appears that Smith was opposed to any form of government that favors Wall Street over Main Street. He was against a government that intervenes in the markets to protect corporate monopolies, and one that promotes the policies of neo-liberalism to the detriment of the pauperized ones of the proletariat. It is difficult to imagine that he would have endorsed tax breaks for the rich. The working class is shortchanged when Wall Street takes precedence over Main Street.

It is obvious that corporate bosses have dragged their feet in merging the ideals of modern capitalism with those of Smith. They were quicker on the draw to socialize poverty. If you look at it one way, capitalist enterprises exploit the working class as scaffolds. Once the objective is achieved, they are discarded. Smith advocated that the consumer is vital to a thriving economy and that they should be treated with respect. The reputed father of capitalism never promoted that the wealth be concentrated in the hands of a few rich corporate bosses.

He advocated that the working class should control prices, not the corporate icons. The competition he referred to was inherent in the production of a variety of products that would be exchanged among the various competing small farmers who lived in the seventeenth century. Smith would most likely not endorse how capitalist opportunists are systematically and savagely destroying every inch

---

24 Korten, "The Betrayal of Adam Smith—Excerpt," Living Economies Forum, http://1ref.us/18.
25 Ibid.

of the world's natural resources in their selfish quest for profit and power. The victims of this misdemeanor have become living epitomes of animated economic disgrace.[26]

"Smith believed that the individual's self-interest, in an environment of similarly motivated individuals, would result in competition. It was this market competition that would provide the goods that society wanted, in the quantities it desired, at prices that it preferred to pay."[27] The final precipitate of such competition would be wealth for the participants. "He summed up the consumer's preeminent position within capitalism by stating, 'Consumption is the sole end and purpose of all production.' However, his knowledge and experience were limited to 18th-century England, so he did not (and could not) foresee the changes and difficulties that would come from the industrial revolution of the 19th century."[28] No matter how distinguished an author may be, one should not read too much into a single account made in a specific situation and at a given point in time

The Industrial Revolution and Communism

The Industrial Revolution got off to a very slow start, and the forecast at the outset was very gloomy. It eventually picked up pace and "increased urbanization of society. As often happens, the people displaced from the land provided a ready source of cheap labor for industry; and industry, in turn, provided the means for increased farm production through mechanization."[29] With the emigration of more and more people to the United States, capitalism took off in America because the land was ripe for that type of system. There was "no feudal society to abolish, and the Civil War in the 1860s destroyed the economic base of the landed aristocracy of the south, encouraging industrialization and setting the stage for economic expansion."[30]

But the Industrial Revolution in England gave birth to the father of communism—Karl Marx. Marx established himself as a "sworn enemy of capitalism, seeing it as the vehicle for the exploitation of workers (the 'proletariat') by the 'bourgeoisie.' Marx believed that capitalism contained the seeds of its own destruction and would inevitably collapse, giving rise"[31] to a state controlled by the working class. This world has never seen a state that is controlled by the people, not even in the United States of America. Marxism settled for a state that controlled the people, in which riches are taken from the rich and redistributed among the poor. By definition, this is socialism. Whereas, communism dictates that everything belongs to the state. Both Marxism and communism have bowed out to modern capitalism.

Investing Overseas

Inequitable wealth distribution forced yet another mutation in capitalism in order to ensure its perpetuation. The problem was that the working class was addicted to consumption, but they lacked

---

26 Ibid.
27 Welch, "Everymoney: Capitalism, Democracy and Global Wealth: Part 1," *Vision*, http://1ref.us/q.
28 Ibid.
29 Ibid.
30 Ibid.
31 Ibid.

the money to indulge. On the other hand, "the wealthy had the money, but did not have the physical capacity to consume their proportionate share of economic production. Therefore the wealthy had to save or invest their excess wealth. But it made no sense to invest domestically to produce shoes if there were already more shoes than they could use."[32]

Capitalism became drunk with success. It had just come out of a stunning victory over communism. With this sweeping victory fresh in its memory, and driven by an insatiable thirst for wealth and power, capitalism began to entertain megalomaniacal ideas of imperial ambitions.

As capitalism went from strength to strength, its presence grew wider and deeper. The stage was set for imperialism to make its dramatic entrance and reshape the economic landscape of the world. This was done more from a capitalistic, rather than a nationalistic perspective. It was now empowered to demonstrate "its ability to displace competing noncapitalistic economic systems."[33] The moment was opportune for it to make its move to consolidate its global grip. It would take wings and fly overseas to institutionalize its absolute dominion. Therefore, in essence, "the imperial age of overseas expansion was, in reality, the internationalization of capitalism."[34] Driven by the twin engines of greed and skullduggery, imperialism swept across the economic landscape of the world like wildfire. On its way to prosperity, a long trail of treasure mixed with blood was left behind. The implications of this move were not only timely but also crucial. It cannot be overstated. The inevitable results led to "the multinational corporation, with its transplantation of production facilities overseas in the inexhaustible search for cheap labor and raw materials."[35] Imperialism became the battering ram to buttress capitalistic claims and ambitions.

Efraim Karsh penned this succinct contribution:

> Throughout history, all imperial powers and aspirants have professed some kind of universal ideology as both a justification of expansion and a means of ensuring the subservience of the conquered peoples: in the case of the Greeks and the Romans it was that of "civilization" vs. "barbarity" … For the seventh-century Arabs it was Islam's universal vision of conquest as epitomized in the Prophet's [Muhammad's] summons to fight the unbelievers wherever they might be found.[36]

Saddam Hussein insisted that the annexation and occupation of Kuwait was done with noble intention. It was done "to eliminate the 'traces of colonialism' in the Middle East so as to expedite the unification of the Arab nation; to promote the liberation of Palestine and Jerusalem … from Jewish-Zionist occupation."[37] Capitalism lures its supporters to its cause by the unsustainable promise to peasants of

---

32 Ibid.
33 Ibid.
34 Ibid.
35 Ibid.
36 Karsh, *Islamic Imperialism: A History*, p. 24.
37 Ibid., p. 182.

relief from a grim and brutish existence to a better life through better paying jobs and equal opportunity to acquire riches, providing they are willing to work hard and take risks. In this manner, the social class is dazzled by the sparkling, yet shallow, promises of self-aggrandizement, early retirement, riches, and power. With the unprecedented inculcation of cable and satellite television in the 1970s, an entire culture found themselves sitting in the "living room" of the entire globe! There is nothing more enticing and compelling in this world than the American dream advertised in living color on television. A face-to-face encounter with the vicissitudes of imperialism is at variance with its commercialized counterpart. It is one thing to see capitalism advertised from overseas and another to be drawn into its entangling web spun by greed and dishonest practices. In short order, capitalistic practices progressively superseded local traditional economic interests.

It didn't take long for third world countries to be swiftly but steadily annexed to the expanding domain of nascent capitalism. It quickly became the hub of the global economic landscape, having embraced almost every nation, kindred, tongue, and people. It is no surprise that the United States of America, the most capitalistic of nations, emerged as its millenarian linchpin and bastion and established the rules by which all other nations would play the game.[38] Free enterprise is the signature and symbol of American prowess. If capitalism sneezed in the United States, the rest of the world said, "God bless you." Nevertheless, the internationalization of capitalism was a debacle. It opened Pandora's box, which resulted in "significant pain and suffering, in the form of the Great Depression of the late 1930s, followed by World War II." These two plagues of society were set in motion by the imperialism of the more powerful nations. This global imprudence of the nineteenth and twentieth centuries, called imperialism, would trigger off a string of wars in third world countries. Not to mention the dramatic altering of the geopolitical landscape and power structures of the day. "During that dark period, when both the economy and liberty itself seemed to hang in the balance, no one could have imagined the economic prosperity to come, as capitalism drove the world economy into the 21st century.[39]

---

38 Welch, "Everymoney: Capitalism, Democracy and Global Wealth: Part 1," *Vision*, http://1ref.us/q.
39 Ibid.

Chapter 4

How Capitalism Perpetuates Poverty

Overview

The central point in this chapter is that the economy will not recover as long as capitalist icons seek to constantly increase their profits at the expense of the working class. Making laborers work longer, harder, faster, for less pay, and in worse conditions will not cut it. The key to economic recovery is to raise minimum wage to living wage. Adam Smith's theory, which capitalist corporations revere, would become a reality: "Give me that which I want, and you shall have this that you want." Give me a decent living wages, brother capitalist, and I will produce and consume all your products. Both the working and capitalist classes will both do well economically if this practice was followed. A paraphrased version of a Winston Churchill quote is given new meaning in this chapter, "Never in the field of human conflict [the global finance industry] has so much been owed by so many to so few."

How Capitalism Breeds Poverty

Pope Francis has recently blamed capitalism for the perpetuation of poverty. Shikha Dalmia, a columnist for the *Washington Examiner,* took an oppositional stance to the pope's position, arguing that he should refrain from demonizing capitalism because it has done far more to turn back the hands of poverty than Catholicism itself.[1]

It is argued energetically, that "by raising productivity and lowering the price of goods, markets certainly help the rich, but they help the poor more. Capitalism's most impressive achievement, Joseph

---

1 Dalmia, "Pope Francis Shouldn't Bite the Hand That Feeds the Catholic Church," *Washington Examiner*, http://1ref.us/19.

Schumpeter noted, was not providing more silk stockings for the Queen, 'but in bringing them within reach of factory girls.'"[2]

Schumpeter has a point that capitalism's most stunning achievement is that goods are brought within striking distance to the common people. But unknowingly, he also unveiled its vulnerability. What is the use of having the goods close enough to reach out and touch if you lack income to buy it? While it is true that productivity is on the rise, the jury is still out as to whether increasing productivity is lowering prices. Perhaps this was what Pope Francis was alluding to.

Historian Deirdre McCloskey argued that "if all the profits of the rich in America were handed over to workers … the workers would only be 30 percent better off. 'But in the last two centuries we're 3,000 percent better off.'"[3]

Nobody is talking about handing over all the profits to the workers, but how about giving them a living wage that they can indulge in some consumption and small investing? Guess what? I believe that if this were to become a reality McCloskey's formula would be reversed in the long run. Consumption would increase, the workers would be 30 percent better off, and the corporations would be 3,000 percent better off! This is not a personal opinion; this is a basic fact of economics. Perhaps this was what Pope Francis was getting at.

The great sentence of a free enterprise society is punctuated by a love affair between the working class and the capitalist class. Capitalism thrives on poverty and on the working class. Therefore, the perpetuation of the miseries of keeping the wages of the working class to a minimum is paramount to its survival. However, it will ultimately be the cause of its demise. Let us consider some mechanisms that must be rigorously maintained in a capitalistic society engaged in the ruthless pursuit of perpetuating poverty.

Low Wages

The flattening of wages is the single most activity that succinctly epitomizes capitalism. This groundbreaking socioeconomic dynamic is the jewel in its crown and the trademark of its pretenses. "To boost their profits, [capitalist] employers have ruthlessly attacked wages, benefits, and working conditions."[4] Such actions amass huge fortunes for employers while, at the same time, perpetuating poverty and the exploitation of the poor by the rich. "Inherent in capitalism has been the maintenance of a sizeable pool of unemployed workers living on the edge of poverty who are desperate for jobs."[5] The ambitious corporate elite can step into this welter of despondence, create the conditions for job competition, flatten wages, and then walk away with the loot. Karl Marx, tapped as the founder of scientific socialism, maintained that the flattening of wages is the pivotal tool used to advance the cause of

---

2 Ibid.
3 Ibid.
4 Wilsdon, "How Capitalism Breeds Poverty," Committee for a Workers' International, http://1ref.us/1a.
5 Ibid.

capitalism. "When this political and economic system is judged by future inhabitants of the planet, this policy will be judged, correctly, as one of the greatest crimes against humanity."[6]

In a capitalist system, the working class is disenfranchised by a political system that favors big corporations. They sit alone at the bottom of the economic strata with bemused indifference. "Worse still, they [these unfortunate victims] have been demonized. Under such conditions, it is no wonder that acts of desperation occur,"[7] which unfortunately result in minorities being viewed with suspicion and disdain through the imprisoning lens of a hostile society that loves to create stereotypes.

The policies of neo-liberalism have hit African Americans and Latinos like a tsunami. Drugs, alcohol, and diseases such as HIV/AIDS are prevalent among these people groups, especially those who live in the inner cities. Without the hope of finding a living-wage job, many occupy their time with less productive pursuits, such as getting into trouble with the law. It is no surprise that of the 2.3 million people incarcerated in 2008, more than one million are African Americans.[8] "It is such conditions that have allowed gangs and violent criminals to terrorize entire communities, events which are distorted by the corporate media to condemn those living in the community."[9]

The way out of this economic dilemma has many competing alternatives. Notwithstanding, many believe the only viable solution is to raise minimum wage high enough to empower the working class to start consuming an ever-rising productivity. People who work for a living should be able to make a living. However, merely raising minimum wage is not enough to combat the greed of capitalism. From 1938 to 2009 the federal minimum wage has been raised twenty-three times,[10] but the cruel harsh reality is that the increasing cost of inflation has outdistanced the more cumbersome increase of minimum wages. Department stores and fast food restaurants raise minimum wage every year for their employees. The only problem is that they are only raising it by five, ten, or fifteen cents! This explains the waning fortunes of a bubble and bust economy for the past three or four decades. The solution is not in raising minimum wage, it is imperative that it be raised to a living wage. This would provide the working class with enough capital to consume goods. In turn, the economy would boom, because when the working class does better, everybody does better.

If the minimum wage were raised to at least $10 an hour, millions would be lifted out of poverty. It is that simple. Taking it a step further, if minimum wage was approximately $12 an hour, consumers would be empowered to purchase more, and the economy would boom to the benefit of all. Then, Adam Smith's theory that capitalist corporations revere would become a reality: "Give me this that I want, and you shall have this that you want." In other words, the working class is saying, "Give me a decent living wage, and I will produce and consume all your merchandise." Both classes mentioned will be well off in a more equitable manner. This is no government handout. This is not taking from the rich to give to the poor. This is giving the working class the living wages they deserve. Therefore, the

---

6   Ibid.
7   Ibid.
8   "Criminal Justice Fact Sheet," NAACP, http://1ref.us/27.
9   Wilsdon, "How Capitalism Breeds Poverty," Committee for a Workers' International, http://1ref.us/1a.
10 "Federal Minimum Wage Increase for 2007, 2008, & 2009," Labor Law Center, http://1ref.us/1b.

accusing finger of "socialism" would not be pointed in its direction. This is about wages that the working class deserves.

Modern corporations are yet to understand a signature principle that was practiced by corporate icons the likes of Carnegie, Ford, Rockefeller, Vanderbilt, and J. P. Morgan. If minimum wage were raised to a living wage, local businesses and corporations would find that their employees would use their increased wages to purchase more. Higher wages also benefit businesses in other ways, such as reducing costly employee turnover, raising productivity, and improving product quality and company reputation. In 2006 CNN commentator Lou Dobbs asserted that "raising the minimum wage isn't simply about the price of labor. It's also about our respect for labor."[11] Prior to the bourgeoisie revolution at the dawn of the twentieth century, there was an even deeper respect for labor. It was not for sale (see chapter 3). But if it is to be sold, it should be done respectably by giving employees a living wage.

Perhaps Adam Smith would turn in his grave if he could see how labor has been degraded and besmirched by corporate capitalists. Henry Ford was one of America's greatest business innovators. He worked his way into American history a century ago. In 1914 he "started an industrial revolution by more than doubling wages to $5 a day—a move that helped build the U.S. middle class and the modern economy."[12] Ford not only paid his employees well enough to buy the automobiles they built, but he kept his employees loyal and productive, which is also very good business. It is not reported that any of his assembly line workers rose to become richer than he was, which is what is seems that some capitalists fear today.

The current federal minimum wage is $7.25 per hour. If a minimum wage worker is employed full-time (forty hours per week for 52 weeks), that worker would earn $15,080 annually.[13] On the other hand, the average annual salary of an employee in the private sector is $60,000, which is half of what the average federal employee makes.[14] The economy would flourish if minimum-waged employers were paid the same as private sector employees. In turn, this gesture would demonstrate the value that corporate America places on working Americans. Whether rich or poor, every individual has the same basic expenses of life. Notwithstanding, doing business as usual continues. Only now restrictions have been increased on eligibility for unemployment benefits, meaning millions are forced to live without any income (see chapter 5). What this means is that tens of millions of workers will see their living standards drop below the poverty line.

Pushed Deeper into Debt

The American working class is not consuming as they used to. "In the US, private consumption has, in recent years, been about 70% of GDP."[15] This speaks volumes, because if there is no consumption,

---

11   Dobbs, "Dobbs: Congress Stiffs Working Americans," CNN, http://1ref.us/1c.
12   "Henry Ford's $5-a-Day Revolution," Ford, http://1ref.us/1d.
13   "What Are the Annual Earnings for a Full-time Minimum Waged Worker?" Center for Poverty Research, http://1ref.us/1e.
14   "Are Federal Workers Overpaid?" FactCheck.org, http://1ref.us/1f.
15   Mody, "G7 Consumption Growth: Implications for Recovery and Global Imbalances," Vox, http://1ref.us/1g.

corporations and capitalism dies. Consumption is on hold and is choking the United States economy. This is why many expert economists are predicting that unless shopping carts start lining up in the checkout lanes, the economy will continue to spiral downward, dropping from a recession into a depression. More consumption means more jobs, more tax revenues, less government spending, and lower national debt. A strong consumer who spends is the solution to the recession. Obviously, consumers cannot spend what they do not possess.[16]

Capitalism in the United States is at a crossroads. How will this great nation cope with this decline in consumption? Will it tenaciously cling to the absurd and unjust conquests of yesterday, or will it answer the clarion call of a glorious tomorrow? Will it in a responsible manner face the stark new limitations that stalk her? Confronted with widespread domestic instability and formidable external challenges, capitalism is becoming a pale reflection of its former self.

Instead of raising the wage of the working class, corporate America has capitalized on the growing enchantment of flattened wages to galvanize huge profits. In a last ditch attempt to regain its footing and to invigorate consumption, this inhumane economic machinery has, in recent years, decided to lend out money and charge consumers heavy interest. This shrewd move mushroomed into a powerful boost and bubble that was short-lived. Its violent backlash has triggered off an unprecedented tidal wave of local, national, and global debt leverage that led to the bubble breaking—and a recession was born.

---

16   Ibid.

Chapter 5

How Government Perpetuates Poverty

Overview

This chapter reveals that welfare programs, federal cuts in public spending, and stimulus packages are the masks capitalism wears to hide its true face—the perpetuation of poverty. Most Americans are unaware that welfare relief first targeted poor white families hit hard by the Great Depression. This chapter discloses the authentic reason why people often are better off on welfare than working a full-time minimum wage job. Reliable statistics lead to the discovery that raising minimum wage decreases the number of welfare dependents. Many propose that a robust economy will result if living wages are given to the working class.

The Preamble to Poverty

There are two diametrically opposed theories concerning poverty and welfare in the United States. According to the first school of thought, welfare is an important government service that helps to reduce poverty in America and abroad. Not so, argues a vast cohort of experts, journalists, and writers. Hunger and poverty is traced back to the lack of buying power. In a broader sense, poverty is the final precipitate of government-endorsed corporate policies skillfully put in place for its perpetuation.

According to the United States Census Bureau, "the number of people living in poverty in America rose by nearly 4 million to 43.6 million in 2009—the largest figure in the 51 years for which poverty estimates are available … the official poverty rate was 14.3 percent, or 1 in 7 of Americans, the highest proportion of the population since 1994."[1]

---

1   MSNBC.com staff, "Record Number of Americans Living in Poverty," NBCNEWS.com, http://1ref.us/1h.

How Government Perpetuates Poverty

Although most people blame hunger on the scarcity of food, Anarudha Mittal, founder of the Oakland Institute, holds that hunger and poverty is traced back to a lack of buying power. In a broader sense poverty is the final precipitate of government-endorsed corporate policies skillfully put in place for its perpetuation. Mittal is on target when she said that "the problem is the scarcity of democracy and the denial of human rights. Hunger is linked to the denial of a living wage to the working poor which forces people to make a choice between having a roof over their heads and food on the table."[2] If these workers were receiving living wages, they would not need handouts or welfare.

"Contrary to what most people believe, hunger is not caused by a shortage of food. World agriculture produces 17 percent more calories per person today than it did 30 years ago, despite a 70 percent [global] population increase. According to the Food and Agriculture Organization (2002), this is enough to provide everyone in the world with at least 2,720 kilocalories per person per day."[3] A person who weighs 150 pounds and lives a normal active lifestyle will need 2,774 kilocalories daily.[4]

I believe that the fingerprints of the existence of God is seen in this seemingly fleeting detail. Mere coincidence does not justify that the calorie count needed for daily survival coincides with what is actually produced. God created the human body. He also arranged for the production of an adequate supply of calories to relieve the need of every creature on planet earth. Presently, resources exist to end worldwide hunger this very moment.

Notwithstanding, there is a huge bend in the road. The problem is that the food resources are continuously been exploited by the few to the detriment of the many. Oxfam International released a report titled "Working for the Few," which stated that "almost half of the world's wealth is now owned by just one percent of the population."[5] Yet they are not reaching out to the poor. Mahatma Gandhi said, "Earth provides enough to satisfy every man's need; but not every man's greed."[6]

Despite the abundance of food in America, almost 100 billion pounds of food is wasted and thrown away every year in this country under the pretense that giving it away to charity is counterproductive in the capitalist world. The idea is "Who will buy stuff if it is given away?" However, there are "700 million hungry human beings in different parts of the world would have gladly accepted this food."[7] Pope Francis made this statement about waste and the struggle of the poor: "Throwing away food is like stealing from the table of the poor and the hungry."[8]

It would be a new day for the global economy if corporate icons would take Adam Smith's economical formula seriously: "Give me that which I want, and you shall have this that you want." If they were to give the working class a living wage, the sagging economy would rebound and the world would

---

2   Souri, "How U.S. Food Aid Policies Perpetuate Poverty," *India Currents,* http://1ref.us/1i.
3   Ibid.
4   "How Many Calories Do I Need a Day?" Fitwise.com, http://1ref.us/1j.
5   Shin, "The 85 Richest People in the World Have as Much Wealth as the 3.5 Billion Poorest," Forbes, http://1ref.us/1k.
6   Gandhi, "Mahatma Gandhi Quotes," Thinkexist.com, http://1ref.us/1l.
7   Siddiqi, "Statistics on Poverty and Food Wastage in America," SoundVision.com, http://1ref.us/1m.
8   McKenna, "Pope Francis Says Wasting Food Is Like Stealing From the Poor," *The Telegraph,* http://1ref.us/1n.

be a much better place to live. This is not some magical wand that will dismiss all the problems of the world in one wish, but it is a down payment of greater things to come.

Brief History of Welfare

People across America suffered when the Great Depression hit the country in the 1930s. "It is estimated that one-fourth of the labor force was unemployed during the worst part of the depression. With many families suffering financial difficulties, the government stepped in to solve the problem and that is where the history of welfare as we know it really began."[9]

However, it is important to point out that this government handout was aimed at poor families of Caucasian descent, not minorities such as African Americans. Although Abraham Lincoln signed the Emancipation Proclamation in 1865, which was a momentous decree that ended the captivity for millions of slaves, during the Great Depression blacks in America were still not free. They were still crippled by the manacles of Jim Crow laws and diplomatic slavery. It is hard to conceive that an ethnic group who did not receive voting rights until 1965 would reap the benefits of a welfare program instituted in the late 1930s.

Blacks were not the beneficiaries of the nascent welfare program. Jesse Jackson said it this way: "Rising tides don't lift all boats, particularly those stuck at the bottom."[10] Let the truth be told. Minorities had to help themselves from the crumbs that fell from the tables of Caucasian Americans. To this day, statistics are signaling that minorities are not consuming the majority of public funding.[11] On this matter there is no opposition. Opponents are mere dissenting voices to this unadulterated truth.

Why Welfare Is Attractive for Minorities

When the economy revived after the Great Depression, compensation for a federal job was much higher than low wage or public sector jobs. On the other hand, public sector jobs enjoyed higher pay than private sector low wage jobs thanks to the bargaining powers of the labor unions. However, federal jobs were off-limits for immigrants, even if they had permanent residence status. Citizenship is a non-negotiable prerequisite to obtaining a federal job. From time immemorial, people of Caucasian ethnicity have had more access to federal and public sector jobs than minorities. This holds true even today. After the Great Depression, most of the Caucasian working class found living wage jobs and were able to get off welfare, proving that living wage jobs are the fastest route to get off welfare.

However, because of the poverty culture, many Caucasian families became complacent and comfortable with welfare and refused to rise with the rising tide. African Americans were intentionally placed on welfare. This created a poverty culture of a mixture of whites, African Americans, and minorities that has been perpetuated to the present day. This pool of desperate workers had no alternative but to work private sector jobs that paid minimal wages. Notwithstanding, they live in the same

---

9   "The History of Welfare," Welfare Information, http://1ref.us/1o.
10 Jackson, "1984 Democratic National Convention Address," American Rhetoric, http://1ref.us/2r.
11 Rank, "Poverty in America Is Mainstream," *The New York Times,* http://1ref.us/3d.

socio-economic niches as those who are working federal and public sector jobs and receiving much higher wages. The cost of living is basically the same for all classes. Tickets for shows on Broadway are the same price for both the working class and the ruling class. Surely, an individual making $16,000 annually should exercise better judgment and leave the Broadway shows to those who can afford it. Unfortunately, there is a thin line between utopia and the reality of that which is practiced. Then, to make matters worse, the government is balancing its national budget on the social conscience of society, looking at every nook and cranny to cut public funding. The results are telling. Unemployment rates are breathing down their neck, credit bureaus are whipping them, socio-economic conditions are strangling them, and increasing poverty is crippling them. A study conducted by the Economic Policy Institute indicated that "some 28% of workers are expected to hold low-wage jobs in 2020 [40 million], roughly the same percentage as in 2010."[12] Low-wage workers are under heavy stress to survive in this country. They are forced to live from paycheck to paycheck.

Because of the added stress of surviving, it is not surprising that the United States Census' 2010 Statistical Report found that citizens of Caucasian descent tend to outlive their minority counterparts. "While the average life expectancy for a Caucasians is 78.9 years (76.5 for a male and 80.3 for a female), the average life expectancy for an African American is 73.8 years (70.2 for a man, 77.2 for a woman). Five years is quite a difference. This gap is thought to be because many black people [and minorities] in America have lower socioeconomic status, meaning less access to income, health care, and education—all factors that effect longevity."[13]

Minimum wage is a shade above federal welfare appropriations. Bear in mind that welfare handouts are given based on the federal compensation plan. Higher income from work does not offset the higher costs of health insurance, taxes, or childcare. Therefore, minorities often are better off on welfare than working a full-time minimum wage job. The welfare system in America is flooded by minorities, not because they are lazy, but because it makes sense in their quest to survive.

In certain states, it pays not to work. A news story by USA Today reported that a single mom with two children in Ohio makes $12,000 more a year on welfare than she would get working a minimum wage job.[14]

The Curse of Welfare

Although welfare was created as the answer to poverty, I believe it is the darkest chapter in the history of the poor and working classes of America. It was a handy façade behind which corporate free enterprise could fully enjoy the delicious fruits of profits. In so doing, corporate America tapped into an unending supply of the pauperized ones. Welfare handouts are the mask capitalism wears to hide its true faces—greed and skullduggery! On the surface, this benevolent social program, like lukewarm

---

12 Waldron, "One in Four American Workers Will Be in Low-Wage Jobs for the Next Decade," Think Progress, http://1ref.us/3t/.
13 Dzado, "2010 Average Life Expectancy by Gender, Race, and Country," Suite, http://1ref.us/2a.
14 Jackson, "Obama to Raise Minimum Wage for Some Federal Workers," USA Today, http://1ref.us/2q.

water, seems so fair, objective, and relaxing. But beneath is a turbulent underlying principle that is spurious and cunningly deceptive. It is no secret that the welfare programs in America have one dark ulterior motive—to perpetuate poverty for centuries to come.

Welfare Perpetuating Poverty

The most common welfare programs in America include "Medicaid, food stamps, family support assistance (AFDC), supplemental security income (SSI), child nutrition programs, refundable portions of earned income tax credits (EITC and HITC) and child tax credit, welfare contingency fund, child care entitlement to States, temporary assistance to needy families [TANF], foster care and adoption assistance, State children's health insurance and veterans pensions."[15]

Many feel that it is virtually impossible for an individual who makes $15,000 annually to break away from the vicious cycle of welfare. Without raising minimum wage, the misfortunes of poverty will be perpetuated in this great nation. Cost of housing, food, child care, and other basic necessities force many to continue living within the system. The thread that runs throughout this book is that a healthy economy rides on the shoulders of living wages.

In 2011 it was reported that "new research from the Republicans on the Senate Budget Committee shows that over the last 5 years, the U.S. has spent about $3.7 trillion on welfare."[16] This adds up to an average amount of $740 billion dollars annually. The growing fear is that the safety net is becoming a hammock that is lulling millions of Americans into laziness and complacency. Instead of handing out Medicaid and Medicare vouchers for seniors and doing away with the minimum wage, Americans should be paid a living wage. I will reiterate my point: the fastest route off welfare is living wages. This was what got Caucasian families off welfare after the Great Depression. America did it before. It can be done again! An individual who works for a living should be able to make a living. If this were the case, there would be no need of a safety net.

"Raising the minimum wage to $10.10 an hour, as many Democrats are proposing in 2014, would reduce the number of people living in poverty by 4.6 million."[17] These reliable statistics lead one to conclude that raising the minimum wage would decrease the number of welfare recipients. Instead of spending billions of dollars to keep people on welfare, the government could use that same money to increase the minimum wage to a living wage, which, according to statistics, would dramatically reduce the number of welfare recipients to a manageable figure.

I feel that somebody is playing politics in this country and is intentionally keeping the working class poor and dependent. Let the truth be told. Capitalism cannot survive without poverty. Our country has no intention of getting people off of welfare because these workers are needed to flip burgers and work other minimum wage jobs that pay an average of $15,000 annually. However, in the same breath, public spending is being cut and services that help the poor, such as social security, health care,

---

15 Polecolaw, "How Much Does Welfare Cost?" Newsvine, http://1ref.us/38.
16 Halper, "Report: U.S. Spent $3.7 Trillion on Welfare Over Last 5 Years," The Weekly Standard, http://1ref.us/2h.
17 Konczal, "Economists Agree: Raising the Minimum Wage Reduces Poverty," *The Washington Post,* http://1ref.us/2x.

public hospitals, public housing, and educational grants and student loans, are being reduced in order to raise the debt ceiling. It is under such conditions that acts of desperation take place and people, especially youth, find themselves stealing or acting out because of stress and frustrations with "the system." The heat of the criminal justice system is turned up on them for breaking the law, and they are thrown in jail. This causes the vicious cycle of the miseries of poverty to continue. All the while, the true perpetrators of this vicious crime cycle walk away unscathed.

Many Americans complain about the waywardness of postmodern youth in the inner cities of this country with their low pants, drugs, and tattoos. However, the primary concern should be who or what drew down those pants. Why is it that rivers of drugs are flowing into the inner cities? What is the driving force behind their tattoos? Show me a youth whose body is pierced and colored with all kinds of tattoos, and I will show you a public school where students are allowed to bring vulgarity into the classroom, but not the Bible. The founding fathers prayed for guidance before signing the Declaration of independence, yet prayer is banned in the public schools. Show me a youth with his pants hanging low, and I will show you a single mother struggling to live a normal life while juggling three low wage jobs. When will she find the time to provide proper guidance and structure to her teenage sons and daughters? Provide these people with jobs that pay a living wage, and then perhaps we can sit down and discuss the low pants, the drugs, and the tattoos. The words of W. E. B. Du Bois are prophetic: "If America fails to lift up her slaves, they will pull her down."[18] We will either lift up these underprivileged families by paying them a living wage, or the pants of their children will keep falling lower and lower until they reach the ground, the drugs will keep flowing, and the body piercings will multiply. We cannot have it both ways.

A Safety Net or a Hammock?

Appearing on national television, Congressman Paul Ryan condemned the safety net of welfare as becoming a hammock that is lulling millions of Americans into laziness and complacency. According to the congressman from Wisconsin, his proposed budget would take poor Americans off welfare. Reality condemns such a naïve mentality and is also a stumbling block for any similar foolish ambitions. There is a narrow gap between the promise of the ideal and the reality of contemporary life. Mr. Ryan should know that this is an empty promise. Capitalism cannot survive without poverty. Taking people off welfare destroys capitalism. If the safety net is removed, it should be replaced by living wages.

Politicians argue that research studies underscore that a significant raise in minimum wage would trigger a ripple effect that would increase the cost of gasoline, automobiles, etc. Economists argue that this would open the door to massive layoffs as companies eliminate low-end positions and consolidate their workforce. It is true that businesses will initially have to eat additional costs generated from such a move to a living wage, but increased consumption by the working class will offset these losses and translate into long-term gains.

---

18 Du Bois, "The Talented Tenth," *The Negro Problem*, p. 45.

If Congress is serious about boosting the economy, they could take the billions of dollars spent to keep people on the three main welfare programs and use the money to increase minimum wage to a living wage. Conservatives claim that raising minimum wage to a living wages will not do anything to help the economy. Here are at least two good things: 1) it will boost the economy because people will have more to spend—$22 billion dollars of business money will be injected into the economy—and it will dramatically reduce the number of welfare recipients to a figure that is manageable.

It is hard to figure out why Congress is against raising the minimum wage from $7.25 to $10.10. Corporations stand to benefit the most. Therefore, making less money cannot be the reason for their objection. As was mentioned earlier, there is a group of millionaires and billionaires in America known as the special interest groups. They have already made their fortunes and can live the rest of their lives comfortable on the interest from their liquid assets. They have two more rivers to cross. First, America must be the undisputed number one military power in the world. It must have the best "hammer," and all other nations must be viewed as "nails." Secondly, the singular message is clear. People who come to America—via the Middle Passage, legal or illegal immigration—are coming to be slaves. This is why today diplomatic slavery, economic inequality, segregated society, social exploitations, unjust levels of the playing field, and the denial of voting rights are stealthily taking roots in the American society.

Stimulus Package and Mortgage Meltdown

The stimulus package for the 2001 recession is evidence that our leading economists on both sides of the aisle are still in denial as to what lies at the core of the economic crisis. Because of the heavy global debt leverage, the working class is no longer buying as much as in previous years. Conscientiously or unconsciously, they are hitting corporate capitalism at the one sweet spot where it is vulnerable.

It is fair to say that the recent recession has forced a drastic slowdown of American consumption. The government was compelled to intervene with two massive stimulus packages to compensate for the reduction in consumer spending. It's all part of a noble effort to keep stores and factories open until consumers kick back in and start spending at prior levels. Most economists argue that "when business cannot or will not invest, the government must step in and fill the void with public investment."[19] This intervention is intended to jump-start a stalled economy.

It was not too long after the stimulus package was released before the underestimated evil in man's nature raised its ugly head. Big banks were bailed out to help with refinancing, loans, and modifications, yet foreclosures reached record levels. It is still a travesty and an uphill struggle to modify and refinance mortgages. These indicators tell a grim story. Could it be that the stimulus package money that was intended to come back to taxpayers in loans, mortgage modifications, foreclosure bailouts, etc., was invested in the markets? Is it possible that the yields from taxpayers' bailout money were used to pay off corporate loans while the principal remained in the treasuries of corporate America? Corporate CEOs are still getting their normal bonuses, yet corporations are downsizing jobs faster

---

19   Welch, "Everymoney: Capitalism, Democracy and Global Wealth: Part 2," *Vision*, http://1ref.us/u.

than the stimulus packages are generating them, and home foreclosure is on the rise (one million every year).²⁰ The list goes on and on.

Bailing out the very same corporations whose flawed administration was the cause of the economic downturn is treating the emergency as one of liquidity. In a press conference in 2009 President Obama said, "We simply can't have a system where we throw good money after bad habits."²¹ Politicians are adamant and recalcitrant in their opposition of socializing wealth. For them this is socialism. On the other hand, socializing poverty gets a free ride. The government takes the taxpayers' wealth and transfers it into the very same private institutions that bludgeoned the economy into a mess because of their greed. How do you like that? I feel that this is the greatest display of human hypocrisy of all times. This is not only wrong, but it is immoral.

"Governments should not bail out banks and speculators but the customers who now have every reason to fear for the future."²² Be mindful, "that wage earners rather than asset owners have faced a 35-year downward pressure on their standard of living. Indeed, the golden age for the salaried worker, as a share of GDP [gross domestic product], was between 1945 and 1973 and not this vaunted age of liberalisation."²³

In the year 2010, there were almost 115 million households in the United States.²⁴ In my opinion, if Congress truly wanted to boost the economy, it should have allocated one million dollars to each of the 115 million tax-paying households in America. Each household would have enough to buy a home, a car, pay for school, start a business, etc. This would in turn pump money back into the economy. Imagine the impact on the United States economy if 115 million cars were sold and 115 million homes were purchased. Add to this the millions upon millions of jobs generated from construction and the setup of new businesses. The capitalist power brokers would give all sorts of reasons why this wouldn't work, including the fact that the working class would not re-invest in the economy but would bank the money or blow it on alcohol and drugs.

It appears that when it comes to socializing wealth, the human nature becomes selfish, but when poverty is socialized that very same nature becomes sanctified. Unfortunately, with capitalism everybody loses except the corporate icons who always end up winning.

If my proposal of giving every household one million dollars were brought before Congress, socialism would be the public outcry because corporate tycoons want to keep the working class poor and hungry. Poverty is capitalism's greatest asset. It is necessary that the working class be kept poor that they have no other alternative but to work for the "slave masters of the twenty-first century." This theory is played out with home foreclosures. It is common knowledge that the banks lose more assets going through a foreclosure than they would if new affordable loans were renegotiated. Banks are reluctant to

---

20   "Foreclosure Statistics," NeighborWorks America, http://1ref.us/2e.
21   "President Obama Holds Press Conference," *The Washington Post,* http://1ref.us/3a.
22   Blond, "Outside View: The End of Capitalism As We Know It?" End Times Report, http://1ref.us/23.
23   Ibid.
24   "How Many Households are in the US?" Wiki Answers, http://1ref.us/2m.

help customers because it is in their best interest to keep homeowners poor and dependent and hungry for employment.

If the government can't give taxpayers one million dollars, I reiterate that the least they can do is give them what they deserve—a living wage. With this increase in income, the working class would be able to increase spending and the economy would boom once again.

Chapter 6

The Poor Will Always Be With You

Overview

Poverty is difficult to relieve when government alone shoulders the responsibility. This is true for the United States welfare system. Only a cooperative effort between the government, community, and churches can effectively relieve poverty. Anything less has a rendezvous with bankruptcy. This chapter discusses questions surrounding the biblical perspective on wealth and poverty. This perspective is of noticeable importance for two reasons. "First, a biblical view of wealth is necessary if we are to live godly lives, avoiding asceticism … and materialism … Second, a biblical view of poverty is essential if we are to fulfill our responsibilities to the poor."[1]

A Biblical View of Poverty

The biblical perspective classifies poverty into four different categories. The first school of thought is that many people became poor because they fell under the yoke of governmental tyranny, fraud, and oppression. Many times governments are the perpetrators of unjust laws and endorse wage policies that result in the exploitation of individuals. As was referred to earlier, a sector of the U.S. population is intentionally kept on welfare. In this manner, they have no other option but to work for an average annual income of $15,000. On top of all of this, politicians, half of whom are millionaires, have the audacity to balance the national budget on the social conscience of society. These congressional policies point in one direction—poverty! It should come as no surprise that 46.5 million Americans, or 15 percent of the population, are living in poverty.[2]

---

1 Anderson, "Wealth and Poverty—A Biblical Perspective," Probe Ministries, http://1ref.us/1u.
2 Hargreaves, "15% of Americans Living in Poverty," CNN Money, http://1ref.us/2k.

The second reason for poverty is that poverty signals that God is enlarging territories for greater blessings. Job was blessed after poverty and destruction. Patiently wait and murmur not. As Paul wrote, "All things work together for good to those who love God" (Rom. 8:28).

The third cause of poverty is laziness, improper habits, and apathy. Many are reluctantly coming to the conclusion that inequality, societal classes, and slavery, be it literal or imaginary, will always be a part of American society. This is the American way. An ethnicity will systematically work for less so that the powers that be can swim in the sea of wealth that is drowning the working class. That is life in these United States. Thus it has been, thus it is, and thus it will continue to be. It is a thing called diplomatic slavery. Unfortunately, the victims of such diplomatic enslavement have become so dependent on food stamps, affordable housing, and welfare payments that they feel naked without these. The sure pathway that leads out of this dilemma is called education. Not only is the Jewish proverb true that "an educated man can never be poor," but, as George Washington Carver said, "Education is the key to unlock the golden door of freedom." Nelson Mandela once said, "Education is the most powerful weapon with which you can use to change the world."[3] If the government and society refuse you an education as they did to George Washington Carver, educate yourself as he did. Why? Education is the single most effective means of reducing poverty.

The wise man Solomon disclosed the fourth reason for poverty hundreds of years ago, "The destruction of the poor is their poverty" (Prov. 10:15). The simplified message of the wise man is that a legitimate cause of poverty is the poverty culture. "Poverty breeds poverty, and the cycle is not easily broken. [Many Americans are guilty as charged.] People who grow up in an impoverished culture usually lack the nutrition and the education that would enable them to be successful in the future."[4]

"An individual who grows up in a culture of poverty is destined for a life of poverty unless something dramatic takes place. Poor nutrition, poor education, poor work habits, and poor family relationships can easily condemn an individual to perpetual poverty."[5]

Poverty and Government

"While government should not have to shoulder the entire responsibility for caring for the poor, it … [should be proactive in] defending the poor and fighting oppression. Government must not shirk its God-given responsibility to defend the poor from injustice. If government will not do this, or if the oppression is coming from the government itself, then Christians must exercise their prophetic voice and speak out against governmental abuse and misuse of power."[6]

In addition to stepping in to defend the poor, government should also step forward to assist in times of misfortune. "Many people slip into poverty through no fault of their own. In these cases, government must help to distribute funds."[7] The disastrous federal response to hurricane Katrina exposed

---

3   "10 Great Quotes About the Value of Education," Everest University Online, http://1ref.us/1p.
4   Anderson, "Wealth and Poverty—A Biblical Perspective," Probe Ministries, http://1ref.us/1u.
5   Ibid.
6   Ibid.
7   Ibid

the incompetence, misjudgment, and ideological blinders on the part of the Federal Emergency Management Agency (FEMA). Unfortunately, the track record is conclusive evidence that government programs are not very impressive. Taxpayers have contributed $40 billion to $50 billion a year from 2001 to 2005 for homeland security, yet "when funding for water works and levees in the gulf region [was] repeatedly cut by an administration that seems determined to undermine the public responsibility for infrastructure in America, despite clear warnings that the infrastructure could not survive a major storm, it seems clear someone is playing politics with the public trust."[8]

Like in the Old Testament, American society is in desperate need of a "means test." If people have true needs, they should be relieved. Laziness and poor work habits should not be rewarded. "Our current welfare system perpetuates poverty by failing to distinguish between those who have legitimate needs and those who need to be admonished in their sin."[9]

There is a "widespread perception that most individuals in poverty are nonwhite" and are consuming the bulk of public funding."[10] This is a myth. "According to the latest Census Bureau numbers, two-thirds of those below the poverty line identified themselves as white—a number that has held rather steady over the past several decades."[11]

It is common knowledge that a savings account is off-limits for a welfare recipient. The welfare money has to be used up, lest its subscribers would become wealthy. To beat the system, some women collect welfare using their maiden names and deposit the handout in their husbands' accounts. Someone will always beat the system to try to get ahead of the game.

Poverty and Public Spending Cuts

United by a common dream that tomorrow will be better than today was what built the greatest American middle class the world has ever known in the twentieth century. However, there has been a recent shift in the economic landscape. The wealthiest are given the greatest help under the mistaken belief that when the wealthy are taken care of the middle class will eventually get their share. It was mentioned earlier that rising tides don't lift all boats, particularly those stuck at the bottom. This trickle-down economics worldview, matched by a good measure of tactical pragmatism, has shortchanged America. It has not only destroyed the middle class, but it has also failed the poor and working classes.

"City, state, and federal politicians have gone on an orgy of cuts to taxes and regulations on the corporations and their rich owners. A big handout has been privatizing public services. This reduces taxes for the rich and allows them to directly profit from those services, resulting in demands for lower wages and cost cutting. This results in lowering of quality services—i.e., few public hospitals, poorer quality public housing, further unemployment and lower wages for those in the community. All these are recipes for further inner-city poverty."[12]

---

8 Adams, "After Katrina Fiasco, Time for Bush to Go," *The Baltimore Sun*, http://1ref.us/1t.
9 Anderson, "Wealth and Poverty—A Biblical Perspective," Probe Ministries, http://1ref.us/1u.
10 Rank, "Poverty in America Is Mainstream," *The New York Times*, http://1ref.us/3d.
11 Ibid.
12 Wilsdon, "How Capitalism Breeds Poverty," Committee for a Workers' International, http://1ref.us/1a.

"This dismantlement of government programs and government spending has been a huge boom for the profits of corporations and the super rich who own the bulk of shares. Now the horrific social consequences of these actions have erupted to the surface."[13] A national and global recession is an eloquent argument that the "chickens" have come home to roost.

There is more. Pure neo-liberalism has a "contract" on America. Under this philosophy all laws that constrain business profits are set aside. This means slashing government programs and laws that do not directly benefit free enterprise. Under the camouflage of "getting government off our backs," corporate-backed politicians and supporters are attacking the rights of labor. They have destroyed vital welfare programs, and "have prided themselves on having shredded the safety net for the poor."[14] Politicians are relentless in denying protection to the most vulnerable citizens in our society—children, youth, and women. They go as far as not protecting the planet itself. The beneficiaries of this idiosyncrasy are a minority of the world's people. The vast majority do not reap the same benefits. The lower and working classes can fearlessly perform high up on the trapeze of life provided that there is a safety net to catch them in the event they fall because of the misfortunes of life. When they reach the end of the rope of opportunities, they hope that their government will be able to support them until they can get on their feet again.

The irony of it all is that productivity is on the rise while wages are declining. Americans are earning less while the costs of education, health care, housing, and gasoline are soaring. "Federal support for low-income people's housing was slashed from $32 billion in 1978 to only $5.7 billion in 1988. That's a decline of more than 80%, when adjusted for inflation. It has since been almost completely eliminated."[15] Furthermore, "funding has been slashed for education at the federal and state levels. As a result, the literacy rate of the U.S. has dropped from 18th to 49th place among the world's nations."[16]

It is inexcusable that our elected officials sit in Washington and enact such ill-conceived regulations and policies. However, what is even more reprehensible is that these same officials turn around and campaign for the votes of the people they hurt and win elections because of campaign promises. The government's irresponsible obsession for cuts in spending is to be likened unto the farmer who decided to save $100 a month by cutting down on the food ration given to his best working horse. He accomplished his goal of saving money, but the horse eventually died from starvation. Congress will accomplish its goal of reducing spending, but I project that the economy will collapse and die in the process!

Poverty and Free Trade

"An essential weapon in the neo-liberal assault has been the demand for free trade. Corporate owners want to be 'free' to operate in any community they want, based on who can guarantee them

---

13 Ibid.
14 Ibid.
15 Ibid.
16 Ibid.

cheaper labor and less restrictions on profit-making. If that means abandoning whole communities and moving operations to a different region or country, so be it."[17]

Corporations were awarded huge tax breaks under the premise that the job creators would generate more jobs. This was the mask capitalism wore to hide its true faces—greed and skullduggery. These huge tax breaks for the rich did generate new jobs, but these were promptly shipped overseas. Fierce competition in global markets compels corporations to attack regulations that threaten their profits or move their firms to countries with less regulations. A report from the U.S. Department of Commerce showed that U.S. companies sliced their workforce in America by 2.9 million during the 2000s. During this same period, overseas employment increased by 2.4 million.[18] This greedy misdemeanor places a monkey wrench in the United States finance industry. Could you imagine Carnegie, Vanderbilt, Rockefeller, E. H. Harriman, James J. Hill, and J. P. Morgan outsourcing American jobs?

In His infinite wisdom, the Creator gave mothers a way to feed their babies. It would be absurd for a mother to commercialize her milk to nurse other babies to the deprivation and neglect of her own child. In a similar fashion, it is betrayal to the American people and unpatriotic to its government for corporations to outsource American jobs for a few lousy bucks! Such practices may bring about quick temporary privilege, but eventually it will sweep the American economy down the slippery slope toward the omega of economic chaos and poverty.

The richest individual in the world is the one who counts all the things money cannot buy. Unfortunately, this rule does not seem to apply to corporate America. The very same people who go on television parading themselves as America's self-appointed guardians of true patriotism are putting profit over patriotism. The most effective manner to address the crisis of job outsourcing is to penalize companies that outsource these jobs and reward those who keep jobs at home.

A Cooperative Effort

It is a critical mistake to assume that government should shoulder the entire responsibility for caring for the poor. Only a cooperative effort between government, business, the community, and churches can effectively relieve poverty.

I recently met a young woman in her late twenties who is working forty hours a week with no benefits. She could hardly take home $300 a week, and yet her weekly rent is $125. Fortunately, under the new Affordable Care Act, come January 1, 2015, large corporations with fifty or more employees will be demanded by law to provide health care insurance for their workers. Before this reform, many of the larger corporations only had partial medical insurance on their workers. If a worker got injured on the job, he or she was covered. But if illness or injury occurred away from the job, there was no coverage.

Here is how Congressional leaders working for the special interest groups (50 percent of whom have membership) plan to get around this law. They will shave down employees' hours to thirty hours a

---

17   Ibid.
18   Lach, "5 Facts About Overseas Outsourcing: Trend Continues to Grow as American Workers Suffer," Center for American Progress, http://1ref.us/2y.

week and change their status to part time. Thus, they will not be obligated to provide health coverage to these workers come January 1, 2015. Let us interpret that, using the aforementioned young lady working forty hours a week. Her hours will be trimmed down to thirty and her status changed to a part-time worker. She will remain without benefits and her take home pay will be one day less. This was the kind of exploitation Karl Marx warned against.

There is nothing new under the sun. The African slaves labored without wages or health care benefits to build America's infrastructure. Millions of their sons and daughters are still doing the same to fill the pockets of corporate America. Dr. Ben Carson's statement that the Affordable Care Act was "the worst thing that has happened in this nation since slavery"[19] demands a stern rebuttal. Dr. Carson seems to be conveniently forgetting that the African slaves had no health care benefits during the time of slavery. Now they have coverage thanks to the Affordable Care Act. How can such a reform be worse than slavery? This nascent law has done something for millions of Americans. It eliminates one aspect of slavery, ensuring that Americans of all ethnicity will no longer have to labor without health care benefits.

The media makes it sound as if the Americans who had zero health care coverage will now get free insurance from the government. However, that is not the case. The government will subsidize the health insurance for these people. Notwithstanding, the corporations will be obligated to come up with more out of pocket for full coverage. They grumble that they will have to eat all the additional costs of the premiums. However, I feel that this is distorting the reality. They are correct that the premiums will go up for full coverage, but the increased costs are subsidized by the government, the corporations, and the working class. The salary for the working class will decrease, but they will take home full health care coverage. Of course, the corporations want to continue doing business as usual, giving the workers the least so that they can get the most.

The Affordable Care Act is one door that the working class, capitalists, and the government can walk through together on the long journey to relieving poverty as a team instead of placing the sole burden of the plight of the poor on the government.[20]

The Playing Field Is Not Level

Studying a comparative chart of the unemployment rate of whites and blacks, it is noticeable that from 1954 to 2013 the unemployment rate among blacks was always double that of their white counterparts, regardless of whom was president.[21] It is evident that slavery (diplomatic or literal), inequality, and exploitation are permanent fixtures in American society. Some people will be slaves. And who do you suppose those slaves will be—the poor? The special interest groups are running the show in America and deciding who is hired and fired.

---

19 Wilstein, "Dr. Ben Carson Calls Obamacare 'Worst Thing Since Slavery' at Values Voter Summit," Mediaite, http://1ref.us/3w.
20 Anderson, "Wealth and Poverty—A Biblical Perspective," Probe Ministries, http://1ref.us/1u.
21 Desilver, "Black Unemployment Rate Is Consistently Twice that of Whites," Pew Research Center, http://1ref.us/29.

There is a saying that in America life is not fair, but opportunity is. But how can opportunity be fair if you are living in an unfair environment where the playing field is not level and unfair people are setting the rules of the game? This is why the poor will always be with us.

Breaking the Poverty Cycle

The poor are always around because individuals, churches, and the community are still in the grandstands watching the government struggle alone in the relief effort. Unless these vital players get down from the grandstands and get on the playing field, the poor will always be with us. "Here is where the church can provide some answers. First, in the area of capital investment, churches should have a benevolent fund in place to help those in need. Christians should reach out to those in poverty by distributing their own financial resources and by supporting ministries working in this area. Such an outreach provides churches with a mechanism to meet the physical needs of the poor as well as a context to meet their spiritual needs.

"A second solution is for Christians to use their gifts and abilities to help those caught in the web of poverty. Doctors can provide health care. Educators can provide literacy and remedial reading programs. Businesspeople can impart job skills.

"This kind of social involvement can also provide opportunities for evangelism. Social action and evangelism often work hand in hand. When we meet people's needs, we often open up opportunities to reach them for Jesus Christ.

"This leads to a third solution. Christian involvement can lead to spiritual conversion. By bringing these people into a relationship with Jesus Christ, we can break the culture of poverty. Second Corinthians 5:17 says that we become new creatures in Jesus Christ. Being born again can improve attitudes and family relationships. It can give new direction and the ability to overcome handicaps and hardships. [The church can help those addicted to alcohol or other drugs to overcome their dependencies. Christians can work to heal broken families. Dealing with these root causes will help solve the poverty problem.]

"A fourth area of Christian involvement is to call people to their biblical task. Proverbs 6:6 says, 'Go to the ant, you sluggard, observe her ways and be wise'; we see here that we are to admonish laziness and poor habits that lead to poverty. In the New Testament, Paul reminds the Thessalonians of their church rule: 'If a man will not work, he shall not eat' (2 Thess. 3:10). Christians should gently but firmly admonish those whose poverty is the result of poor work habits to begin taking responsibility for their own lives."[22]

---

22 Wilsdon, "How Capitalism Breeds Poverty," Committee for a Workers' International, http://1ref.us/1a.

Chapter 7

A Blessing in Disguise

Overview

This chapter exposes how a recession is used to downsize the workforce, cut public spending, and raise taxes and tolls. While many would say there's nothing good about a tanking economy, this chapter focuses on the brighter side of a recession. American citizens should use the recession as a frame of reference to redefine the old version of the American Dream and begin to live within their means. This would force corporate America to come to the table and raise the minimum wage to a living wage. Until that happens, the chapter offers concrete suggestions as to how consumers can survive the crisis of an economic recession.

The Recession Myth

Since 2010 to the present there has been a slow but steady growth in consumer confidence, in private sector jobs, in the national gross domestic product (GDP), and in real estate purchases, and a decrease in unemployment claims. These are strong indicators that the United States economy is on its way to recovery and that the recent 2001 recession is on a decline. If indeed the recession is gaining momentum, why is it that CEO's are still the beneficiaries of fat bonuses and corporations are raking in astronomical profits? Furthermore, it is interesting to note that during the recessions of 1974, 1980, 1982, and 1990, churches reported increases in church revenue.[1] Yet the media waves are saturated with the voices of economic prophets of gloom and doom, declaring that the recession is deepening. They go as far as to predict that it is on the verge of a double dipping.

---

1 Ronsvalle, "Church Member Giving in Recession Years: 1974, 1980, 1982 and 1990," Empty Tomb, Inc., http://1ref.us/3g.

Economic Recession: A Blessing in Disguise?

There are those who stand in opposition to this theory. There are some who feel that recessions are skillfully and intentionally put in place by special interest groups who stand to benefit the most. These elite groups hold the handle of the economic dagger. If they sneeze, the media and politicians say, "God bless you." If they say there is a recession, there is one, even if there is none. Under the camouflage of a recession, governors manipulate state budgets as the bargaining tool to disable and hamstring the power of collective bargaining. I personally believe that recessions are the mask politicians wear to hide their true faces, which is to cut public spending and the deficit, and raise taxes and tolls.

A Blessing in Disguise

However, in spite of this, there is a surprising blessing concealed in the bosom of an economic downturn. If the working class plays it right, they can emerge as the victors. "While there is no such thing as a good recession, it doesn't have to cause unmitigated gloom and despondency."[2] In a recession, reduced funds coerce the working class to revert to a survival mode. They limit their spending and activities to things that are only necessary. In this sense, a recession can be a blessing in disguise. During a time of economic crunch, people are worried about losing their jobs. Therefore, they avoid trouble and live healthier to avoid from getting laid off. In a paper titled "Healthy Living in Hard Times, Christopher Ruhm, a professor of economics at the University of North Carolina, "suggests that in America during the recession in the 1990s, smoking, particularly among heavy users, declined by 5 per cent."[3]

Research reveals that people tend to neglect caring for themselves and their families when there is a boom in the economy. It is during economic downturns that people find more time to visit with family, such as elderly relatives and their children. Many people try to eat healthier so as to not get sick and the roads are also less crowded because gasoline prices are high, which has a positive environmental effect.[4]

There are other benefits to be harnessed from an economic downturn. Consumption is the motor that drives capitalism at record-breaking speed along the highway of success and prosperity. Like a fish cannot survive out of water, capitalism will not survive long out of the friendly confines of consumption. If there is no consumption, capitalism dies. Therefore, it is during a recession that the hand of capitalist corporations is forced to drop prices on food, clothing, and gasoline. With spending at its all-time low, corporate empires offer special deals in a last ditch effort to spark public spending. The moment is opportune to tap into this resource and take advantage of these unprecedented offers.

Redefining the American Dream (Living Beyond Debt)

No matter how distasteful or damaging, recessions force many consumers to take a long, hard look at their personal expenses. Here are some tips that hopefully will be useful to consumers who have to live through a recession.

---

2 Thomson, "Why the Recession Is a Blessing in Disguise," *Bangladesh News*, http://1ref.us/3p.
3 Ibid.
4 Ibid.

Consumers should redefine the American Dream. The old version of the American Dream advertised on television is that one's self-worth is measured according to the standard of consumption. You are living the American Dream if you drive the right car, live in the right kind of neighborhood, or dress a certain way. This was what got Americans in trouble in the first place. One of the greatest blessings of an economic downturn is that the working class has no option but to redefine the American Dream to mean, "Living within our means."

Let us take a look at the Amish community. They employ horse-drawn power to till the soil because they know that tractors and bulldozers destroy top soil and increase the chance for soil erosion and desertification. "In comparison to our fast-paced society, the simpler, family-centered Amish way of life holds a special fascination…. The more traditional groups are called 'old 'order'. They do not permit electricity or telephones in their homes. By restricting access to television, radio, and telephones, the Amish are better able to keep the modern world from intruding into their home life."[5]

Our society would be better off during a recession if we were to live as the Amish. Our focus should be more on private gardening. Dressing should be more modest. And public transportation should be used more. Such actions would in turn coerce corporations and the government to reconsider and amend their wayward trends. Notwithstanding, consumers are not quite ready yet to start churning butter or darning socks. They don't have the time or skills. And in today's high-tech world such a lifestyle is considered boring. The problem is that America is addicted to consumption and keeps on buying without money and regardless of the price.

Consumers should avoid the debt trap like leprosy. Debt is corporate America's invention, tailor-made to perpetuate poverty and dependence. All the while it simultaneously allows the working class to increase their level of consumption. The average American citizen must be smart during an economic crisis. More and more people are turning to auction-based or for-sale-by-owner shopping, but even here prices can be steep.

Consumers should keep on spending on necessary things. Being in the middle of an economic downturn is not the moment to reinvent the wheel. While it is arguable that the natural tendency is for the oppressed to be more frugal in their spending, they must not vindictively shy away from any further consumption practices. This was what triggered the recession in the first place. One has to be "wise as serpents and harmless as doves" (Matt. 10:16). It would serve no earthly good if anger about past exploitation provokes a total halt in consumer spending. Killing the bee that stung you does not alleviate the pain from the sting. A sudden halt in spending would kill corporations and destroy any chance for the survival of the working class. None can survive without the other. Prolonging the consumer-corporate relationship in the long run is beneficial to the working class. It is during a recession that the financial vision of corporate bosses is fine-tuned to see and come to terms with the importance of consumers in the economic industry. It is vital for the survival of the United States economy that American consumers back up and reclaim their rightful place in the checkout lane. However, I say this

---

5   "Amish and the Plain People." LancasterPA.com, http://1ref.us/1r.

with a word of caution, because consumers should not spend what they don't have. If corporations would raise the minimum wage to a living wage, consumers would be able to consume more, which would boost the corporations' profits.

Consumers should sit and wait for their change to come. Corporate capitalists will eventually be brought to their knees. They will be forced to sit around the table of compromise and negotiate raising the average salaries of the working class to a decent level that can afford them a dignified existence. Consumption most likely will resume. Needless to say, this will boost the economy.

Here is the conclusion of this matter. While many would say there's nothing good about a tanking economy, there is a brighter side of a recession. When the years have rolled by and we think back to the recession of 2001, I hope we will be able to tell our children and grandchildren that the economic downturn made a dramatic recovery because the citizens of America were able to redefine the old version of the American Dream and began to live within their means.

Chapter 8

The Decline of Capitalism

Part 1

Overview

The greatest challenge posed for the champions of free enterprise is to figure out how to save capitalism from its worst inherent aspects and most damaging tendencies. This chapter will examine the Enron fiasco and the inherent covert sins of corporate capitalism. This ignited a volcanic eruption of long-suppressed popular common passions and desires of the American people. It also exposed why capitalism is an economic success but a sociological failure. In this chapter the focus is on the first three of five reasons why capitalism is on the decline.

Enron: Symbol of Declining Capitalism

A system or organization begins to decline the moment its constituency discovers that its executives are indulging in habitual practices of presumptuous hypocrisies. The "robber barons" of the nineteenth century were primarily driven by a desire to build up their own economic fortresses. The building up of America's economic infrastructure was only incidental rather than the underlying impetus of the work of such people as Carnegie, Vanderbilt, and Rockefeller. "Patriotism may be the last refuge for the scoundrel, but the 'malefactors of great wealth' at least saw themselves as master builders of America."[1]

It was an honorable rule among gentlemen who were traveling aboard a ship that if the boat went down the women and children should be first in the lifeboat, and the captain would go down with the ship. "But, at Enron, the women and children were locked in steerage, so they would not interfere as

---

1   Buchanan, "Enron and the Decline of Capitalism," The American Cause, http://1ref.us/25.

The Decline of Capitalism: Part 1

captain and crew [Enron executives] hauled the ship's safe, with all the passengers' valuables, into the lifeboats and shoved off."[2]

At the time of its collapse, Enron boasted then of being the seventh largest United States corporation, a rival only to General Motors and General Electric. Its sudden breakdown sent shivers through the country's financial industry and exposed corporate capitalism for what it truly is—a hardnosed economic industry that exploits the working class in exchange for huge exorbitant capital profits. Enron "represents a new 'casino capitalism,' where men make millions—not by creating new products, but by gaming the system."[3] Bankers and financiers generated fictitious wealth in the form of financial "products" wrapped in beautiful packages and sold for real money to economically illiterate ordinary citizens.

The Enron fiasco ignited a volcanic eruption of long-suppressed common passions and desires of the American people. In no uncertain terms, they expressed their fatigue of the abuses of capitalism. Corporate greed, stuck in the neck of the "funnel" of the finance industry, allows little or no capital to trickle down to the middle and lower classes as is stipulated in "Reaganomics." To top it off, the increased use of computers in business meant that more work could be done with a reduced work force. During this time, productivity rose, wages began to plateau, and corporations and executives bathed themselves in wealth generated from huge profits. These factors prompted the American people to lose faith, trust, and belief in the conventional system.

Richard Wolff describes this financial top prize for corporate America: "Employers' profits have gone wild, and all the people who get their fingers on employers profits—the professionals who sing the songs they like to hear, the shareholders who get a piece of the action on each company's profits—have enjoyed a bonanza over the last thirty years.

"The only thing more profitable than simply making the money off the worker is handling this exploding bundle of profits—packaging and repackaging it, lending it and borrowing it, and inventing new mechanisms for doing all that. That's called the finance industry, and they have stumbled all over themselves to get a hold of a piece of this immense pot of profit."[4]

The Amorality of Capitalism

Perhaps capitalism's greatest nemesis, and why its future prospects are bleak, is its lack of concern with who should get what, only with who has what. It is unprincipled and immoral in both theory and practice because it "puts the importance of profit and wealth accumulation before the interests and human rights of people, namely the laboring class." Therefore, it is powerless to cast moral judgment, as well as unable to address injustice. Capitalism can only thrive in heterogeneous religious, economic, racial, and religious culture found in countries like America. It is only in countries like America, where

---
2   Ibid.
3   Ibid.
4   Wolff, "Capitalism Hits the Fan," AlterNet, http://1ref.us/3x.

the economy does not favor one group's morality to the estrangement of the others, that capitalism can take wing and fly.[5]

Capitalism sits on top of the global economic strata after the fall of the USSR, the transformation of China, and the embracing of a free market economy by the socialist parties of Western Europe. If indeed almost the entire globe embraces some form of capitalism,[6] then global recession most likely is a rejection of such free enterprise society. More and more global citizens are reversing capitalism's motto. People are more concerned with who gets what rather than with who has what. The citizens of the world are asserting their desire to live in a moral society that harnesses the best economic principles from both capitalism and socialism.

Capitalism's principal weaknesses are its inability to cast moral judgment and its "values and morality that determine their way of living and doing business. It is wayward personal motivation and individual and collective selfishness that distorts and perverts the system."[7] Free enterprise is an economic success but a sociological failure. Therefore, it is reduced to an agglomeration of politically driven entities united only by the overarching factors of production, consumption, exploitation, and greed.

Negative Impact on the Weaker Nations

Former Wall Street executive David Driver, and most critics of capitalism, argues that America has "one of the most pro-business, inequitable, and inhumane socioeconomic systems in the industrialized world … It certainly does not benefit the average citizen, [nor] does it benefit the country as a whole."[8] "Capitalism has always been a controversial economic system: it is selfish and unfairly favors the strong, say its critics; it primarily benefits the prosperous West, invariably at the expense of poorer nations; and its huge profits go to multinational corporations, to the detriment of smaller and weaker companies."[9]

More and more global economists are in accord with Michel Beaud, author of *A History of Capitalism, 1500–2000*, when he wrote, "The powers which dominate human society threaten the integrity of man as well as the integrity of the world. The dynamics of capitalism contribute greatly to this process."[10] "At the same time, a so-called 'third' world (because it belonged neither to the prospering capitalistic bloc of nations nor to the communist bloc) was being born through the decolonization process. As the world's dominant capitalistic economies increased their control over economic production and trade, the third world served mainly as a source of raw materials and cheap labor."[11]

The retreat of the colonial powers left in its wake a long trail of civil unrest, escalating violence, and civil wars—particularly in Africa. All "across vast stretches of Africa, diamonds fuel war. Diamonds are so lucrative for predatory governments and marauding rebels that war has become a useful cover

---

5   "Profit Over People: The Immorality of Capitalism," Daily Kos, http://1ref.us/3c.
6   Welch, "Everymoney: Capitalism, Democracy and Global Wealth: Part 1," *Vision*, http://1ref.us/q.
7   Meakin, "The Achilles' Heel of Capitalism," *Vision*, http://1ref.us/s.
8   Wilsdon, "How Capitalism Breeds Poverty," Committee for a Workers' International, http://1ref.us/1a.
9   Meakin, "The Achilles' Heel of Capitalism," *Vision*, http://1ref.us/s.
10 Welch, "Everymoney: Capitalism, Democracy and Global Wealth: Part 3," *Vision*, http://1ref.us/12.
11 Welch, "Everymoney: Capitalism, Democracy and Global Wealth: Part 2," *Vision*, http://1ref.us/u.

The Decline of Capitalism: Part 1 55

for hugely profitable smuggling enterprises. But for millions of Africans who happen to get in the way, diamonds are agents of terror."[12] "In Angola, Congo or Sierra Leone, the glittering stones have become agents of slave labor, murder, dismemberment, mass homelessness and wholesale economic collapse."[13]

"War within nations has continued to be a scourge. According to *The Economist* (May 24, 2003), 'almost all wars are now civil wars. Many of the causes are economic.' The special report examined a World Bank study and concluded that 'the best predictors of civil war are low average incomes, low growth, and a high dependence on exports of primary products such as oil or diamonds.' The article also noted that 'the most striking common factor among war-prone countries is their poverty. Rich countries almost never suffer civil war, and middle-income countries rarely. But the poorest one-sixth of humanity endures four-fifths of the world's civil wars.'"[14]

These tales are but the tip of a huge iceberg of atrocities hidden away in the dark evil recesses of unbridled capitalism. It is reported that capitalism is the greatest crime of all times. The apostle James adds this to the discussion, "And a final word to you arrogant rich: Take some lessons in lament. You'll need buckets for the tears when the crash comes upon you. Your money is corrupt and your fine clothes stink. Your greedy luxuries are a cancer in your gut, destroying your life from within. You thought you were piling up wealth. What you've piled up is judgment. All the workers you've exploited and cheated cry out for judgment. The groans of the workers you used and abused are a roar in the ears of the Master Avenger. You've looted the earth and lived it up. But all you'll have to show for it is a fatter than usual corpse. In fact, what you've done is condemn and murder perfectly good persons, who stand there and take it" (James 5:1–6, MSG). And Paul was not in error when he wrote, "For the love of money is the root of all evil" (1 Tim. 6:10, KJV).

Then there is the funnel effect of capitalism. Stuck at the neck of the economical funnel, capitalism absorbs all that flows from above and beneath. "From a Christian perspective, capitalism is also ethically troubling. It not only recognizes greed, it baptizes and catechizes it, too. Gordon Gekko in Oliver Stone's 1987 movie, *Wall Street,* said it best: 'Greed is good!'"[15]

"The unequal distribution of wealth and income is a disquieting characteristic of global capitalism. French historian Michel Beaud believes that current globalization is polarized, unequal and asymmetric, and that it has resulted in deepening 'inequality between the well-off, rich, and extremely rich, compared to the poor and very poor.'"[16] The *Los Angeles Times* reported the findings of a new study that stated that "the wealth gap between the top 1% and the bottom 99% in the U.S. is as wide as it's been in nearly 100 years."[17] "As a point of reference, *Forbes* magazine (October 13, 1997) reported that the United States had 170 billionaires in 1997, compared to 13 in 1982.... income was disproportionally concentrated in the hands of a small percentage of American families, and the average American 'had

---

12   Harden, "Africa's Diamond Wars," *The New York Times,* http://1ref.us/2i.
13   Harden, "Africa's Gems: Warfare's Best Friend," *The New York Times,* http://1ref.us/2j.
14   Welch, "Everymoney: Capitalism, Democracy and Global Wealth: Part 2," *Vision,* http://1ref.us/u.
15   Larson, "Capitalism: What Were Its Moral Strengths and Weaknesses? Part 1," *Spectrum,* http://1ref.us/r.
16   Welch, "Everymoney: Capitalism, Democracy and Global Wealth: Part 2," *Vision,* http://1ref.us/u.
17   Stewart, "Income Gap Between Rich and Poor is Biggest in a Century," *Los Angeles Times,* http://1ref.us/3n.

mortgaged himself up to his neck [and] had extended his resources dangerously under the temptation of installment buying.'"[18] A similar situation preceded the Great Depression of the 1920s.

Some feel that free markets turn unrestrained greed into socially optimal outcomes. But by definition, greed is the love of money and, as we already read, "the love of money is the root of all evil (1 Tim. 6:10, KJV). Throughout history and today the love of money has provoked wars, the scouring of the entire surface of the planet for resources and the acceleration of global warming, balancing the national budget on social conscience of society, drastic cuts in public spending, the perpetuation of poverty through welfare, flattened wages (cheap labor), tax breaks for the wealthy who don't need it, and predatory loans and stimulus packages that bail out those who got us into the mess in the first place.

As was mentioned in this chapter, violence often erupts as citizens push back against the abuses of corporations. Beginning in the 1950s and continuing through the 80s, in Latin America millions of poor indigenous and mestizos who had been oppressed for hundreds of years found their strength in the streets and provided an audience for social preachers and activists of all hues.[19] This phenomenon was known as *La Teología de la Liberación* (Liberation Theology). These universal revolts were violent backlashes from a deeply frustrated citizenry who were reluctant to come to terms with the self-serving imperialistic policies of capitalism. More than anyone else, the Latinos who took a stand for what they believed in are responsible for the death or the killing of neo-liberalism in Latin America.

---

18   Welch, "Everymoney: Capitalism, Democracy and Global Wealth: Part 2," *Vision,* http://1ref.us/u.
19   "Liberation Theology," Wikipedia, http://1ref.us/2z.

Chapter 9

Part 2

Overview

Two more social conditions contributing to the decline of capitalism are presented in this chapter: changing times and the changing climate. This chapter will answer the following questions. Is the era of "growth" behind us? In a world that has well defined physical limits, like peak oil, peak natural gas, lack of fresh water, depleted fisheries, melting icecaps, and rising global temperatures, how much longer can the engine of capitalism keep running on the resources that remain? Or is it already stalled? Most importantly, *is capitalism even compatible with democracy? If we have to choose, which is more important?* Discover why Christians, the stewards of the earth, should be diametrically opposed to those who are systematically destroying the earth in relentless pursuit of profit.

Changing Times

"We are living during one of the greatest *turning point* in history, in which a system that has just finished colonizing the entire planet is already facing its imminent demise. Like the Babylonian, Mayan, and Roman Empires before it, now capitalism, seemingly secure in its global triumph, is in fact crumbling before our very eyes, and nothing can reverse the deterioration."[1] While a 500-year-old economic system is dying, another is in the process of been ushered in.

Is It the Best of Times or the Worst of Times?

Francis Bacon, an English statesman and philosopher, said, "He that will not apply new remedies must expect new evils."[2] If you want something you don't have, then you must do something you've

---
1 Knight, "Part 5. Conclusion: The World We Are Building," End of Capitalism, http://1ref.us/2w
2 Bacon, Brainy Quote, http://1ref.us/1z.

never done before. Corporate America should have figured it out by now that minimum wages is not the way to economic prosperity. Yet they continue with the same failing economic policies. According to Einstein, "doing the same thing over and over again and expecting different results" is the definition of insanity.[3]

Global recession signals a clear singular universal message that the failing worldwide economy can no longer fly on the weakening wings of conventional capitalism. The capitalist creed of getting what you can is no longer charitable to the working class who navigate the turbulent economic rapids of the twenty-first century. Capitalism is not a monolithic system. It is composed of varying strands of components and ramifications. A predominating idea at any given time is controlled by a series of variables and perceived needs.

For example, following World War II, "the world desperately needed monetary stability, economic expansion, and a regime that would encourage free trade."[4] The 1944 Bretton Woods Conference introduced the International Monetary Fund (IMF) and the World Bank to meet this pressing global financial need. This shrewd economic move is an often-overlooked historical turning point that shaped the economic landscape that probably saved the day for capitalism. John Maynard Keynes pushed for a worldwide supranational central bank that would handle an international monetary system in which the global economies would feed off of each other.[5] In such a system it is required that "both surplus and deficit economies to self-correct rather than put the burden solely on deficit economies to deflate."[6] The motto of the Three Musketeers, "All for one and one for all," summarizes how this bank functions.

If modern global economies are seeing a clear economic path before them, it is because they stand on the solid framework of this postwar financial architecture, which remains in place to this day. No sooner had the ink dried on the paper of the agreement than it fell and bowed out to floating exchange rates. It has long since become a relic of the past. The times have changed, and the very same global economic conditions that prevailed in 1944 have returned with more dire repercussions. "A chorus of voices increasingly calls for reforms more in keeping with the particular needs of today's world: different circumstances dictate alterations in the way capitalism functions."[7] It would do us well to take a lesson from the economic pages of our formidable predecessors.

National and global recessions are conclusive evidence that there is a global push back on capitalism as it is. It is evident that "Reaganomics" is an economical "pill" the citizens of the world are definitely not swallowing. The real challenge is not to totally eradicate capitalism but to come up with a financial plan that will effectively deal with this economic fiasco that is imploding and exploding locally and globally. Addressing the downturn in the United States economy will require corporate America, the federal government, and Main Street to make substantial changes to how they do business. There is

---

3   Einstein, Brainy Quote, http://1ref.us/2c.
4   Welch, "Everymoney: Capitalism, Democracy and Global Wealth: Part 3," *Vision*, http://1ref.us/12.
5   Ibid.
6   Ibid.
7   Ibid.

an urgent need to reinvest in the working class, which is who drives the economy. If businesses were to take this approach, they would be more competitive and productive.

"There are plenty of reasons, then, to conclude that capitalism today has serious flaws in the way it works, rendering it a far-from-ideal economic system. We see that it was not just Marx who predicted its eventual collapse: today numerous voices are raised in protest that the system needs to be fundamentally changed."[8] Let us look at another vital change.

Changing Climate

Some of those changed circumstances include the modern-day malaise of global warming, now almost universally understood to be vividly spurred on by human activity. Environmentalists are in accord that the workings of capitalism have to be urgently harnessed and modified if global catastrophe is to be averted.

Dan DiMaggio and Phillip Locker make the point that it is virtually impossible to stop global warming unless capitalist corporations come on board. Wherever markets are found, there is a potential for profit. This naturally spurs competition between competitors to generate a profit. Businesses know that to keep increasing their profit margin they must keep expanding and growing. All the while, more and more natural resources are used, and the planet suffers.[9]

"The growing productive capacity then reaches *industrial* levels, such that to remain competitive companies must produce not hundreds, but millions, of identical commodities, requiring *factories,* global lines of *distribution,* and huge quantities of readily-available *energy.*"[10] It is by far more economically viable that corporations and enterprises produce a variety of products instead of everybody producing identical goods and fighting for the same sales. This allows a greater cross section for marketing merchandise and equitable prosperity to all, rather than operating under the "survival of the fittest" mentality.

The demands on the ecosystem to keep the wheels of capitalism turning are substantial and are a threat to our planet. The probability of global warming is more real than ever. There is a sense in the air of a foreboding doom that stalks the natural resources of our planet. Governments have failed to act and put an end to all this senseless plundering and pillaging of the earth's natural resources because they are endorsing the ambitions of greedy corporations.

"Further, the degree of international cooperation needed to tackle global climate change is impossible under capitalism. The fierce competition between corporations is mirrored in the relationship between countries. The major capitalist powers are engaged in a relentless struggle over markets, resources, and spheres of influence. Big business sees the environment as just another resource to be used

---

8   Ibid.
9   Locker, "Global Capitalism = Global Warming—The Case for Socialism," Socialist Alternative, http://1ref.us/32.
10 "Who Is the Real Capitalism?" Waspadafurqon's Blog, http://1ref.us/3v.

in the interests of making profits."[11] The environment is like a popcorn stand that businesses pass by on the way to the main arena of generating profits.

Capitalism relies on heavy amounts of energy, resources, and human labor. These are then "commodified, or turned into property to be bought and sold on the market."[12] All operations of "the capitalist machine—from resource extraction, to production, to distribution, to consumption, and finally to waste—is a linear system on a finite planet, which by definition cannot be sustainable."[13] In order to keep pace with the "colossal rate of production" over the past decades "the entire surface of the planet [has been] scoured for resources." [14] This is why the Amazon rainforest in Brazil is being pillaged for lumber and why thousands of acres of forest are disappearing.[15] And sadly, nobody is paying attention to reforestation. Consequently, the carbon dioxide and oxygen cycles are disrupted because of the absence of trees to convert carbon dioxide into oxygen, which is a byproduct of photosynthesis.

A constantly growing economy requires an unsustainable level of consumption of the world's natural resources—oil, minerals, water, plants, and animals. A depletion of the earth's oil supply is perhaps capitalism's worst nightmare. Many of the earth's resources are renewable and can be replaced. If a tree dies, a new one can be planted. Animals can be bred to create offspring. However, there are some resources essential to the capitalist machine that are nonrenewable. Oil is a prime example that offers no alternative for businesses.

America is addicted to oil. "In fact, including tractors, chemicals, packaging, distribution, and cooking, *every single calorie of food in the United States requires at least 10 calories of fossil fuel energy to bring that food to the plate.*"[16] Likewise, further investigation would disclose that nearly everything we consume has at least some component made from oil. It is projected that oil now powers 95 percent of all transportation.[17]

In the case of a sudden oil shortage, the industrial economy would grind to a halt. The military, which is one of the largest consumers of oil, would also be crippled. Here is capitalism's greatest dilemma and why it is on the decline. Oil, which is the most important of the three fuels to corporate America, appears to be the first to enter decline. John the Revelator predicts a foreboding doom that stalks and haunts capitalism—the drying up of the river Euphrates (Rev. 16:12). "Holding true to the symbolic nature of the book of Revelation, some biblical exponents are in accord that 'John [the Revelator] does not here refer to a literal river, or to the drying up of its literal waters.'"[18] A unique and distinct interpretation of the drying up of the Euphrates could be the literal depletion of the oil supply in the Middle East.

---

11 Locker, "Global Capitalism = Global Warming—The Case for Socialism," Socialist Alternative, http://1ref.us/32.
12 Knight, "Part 3: Why Is It Breaking Down?" End of Capitalism, http://1ref.us/2v.
13 Ibid.
14 Ibid.
15 "Deforestation in Brazil," Wikipedia, http://1ref.us/28.
16 Knight, "Part 3: Why Is It Breaking Down?" End of Capitalism, http://1ref.us/2v.
17 Ibid.
18 Nichol, ed., *Seventh-day Adventist Bible Commentary*, vol. 7, p. 843.

"The world could start to run out of oil in the next ten years, sparking soaring energy prices and a rush for even more polluting fossil fuels, an influential new study by the UK Energy Research Council has warned."[19] There are two schools of thoughts concerning the exact date when the world will begin to see a decline in oil production. There are those who contend that this will not become a reality until after 2030. Notwithstanding, some experts are warning that this grim prediction could become a reality as early as 2020.[20]

According to a growing chorus of geologists, there is a shortage of oil in the global community today. It's time to start asking the tough questions that have been put off for far too long. For example, is the era of "growth" behind us? In a world that has well-defined physical limits—the likes of peak oil, peak natural gas, lack of fresh water, depleted fisheries, melting icecaps, and rising global temperatures—how much longer can the engine of capitalism keep running on the resources that remain? Can it last a decade? Or is it already stalled?[21]

"While scientific research needs to continue [on global warming], it is clear from the accumulated evidence that the increasing emission of destructive gasses, the massive destruction of the American rain forests, and the depletion of the protective mantel of ozone (the so-called greenhouse effect), are all threatening the earth's eco-system."[22] The irresponsible pursuit of greed is taking a heavy toll on the earth's natural resources.

The apostle Paul wrote that the entire "creation groans and labors with birth pangs" (Rom. 8:22). God is the undisputed Creator of this planet. He is not pleased when His creatures destroy His creation, and in the end, those who destroy the earth will be destroyed (Rev. 11:18). Christians are the stewards of the earth. Therefore, they should be in diametric opposition to those who are systematically destroying the earth. The church should be at the vanguard denouncing this destructive rampage of economical schizophrenia. This open disregard for human life on this planet must be confronted and nipped in the bud. Let us be sure that we are doing our best to protect the natural resources that God has given us.

---

19 Gray, "Era of Cheap, Easy Oil Is Over, Warns Study," *The Telegraph*, http://1ref.us/2g.
20 Ibid.
21 Knight, "Part 1. Is This the End of Capitalism?" End of Capitalism, http://1ref.us/2u.
22 "Stewardship of the Environment," Seventh-day Adventist Church, http://1ref.us/3l.

Chapter 10

Part 3

Overview

In a wide-ranging fashion, this chapter leaves no stone unturned to show why postmodernism is at variance with the dynamos of capitalism and why this will eventually lead to its demise. This chapter not only discloses the one area where capitalism is most vulnerable, but it also addresses why it is social, economic, and political suicide to underestimate the power of the working class. Globally, their cause is getting stronger, and capitalism is declining.

The Postmodern Impact

"The trunk of the tree of postmodernism is the proposition that 'truth' is not absolute (or if it is, it can't be known). That is, 'truth' does not transcend cultures or eras. 'Truth' is what an individual or group (such as community, culture, society, club, nation) makes it. Consequently, what is 'true' for one person may not be for another."[1]

Postmodernism is described by one writer as an "enormous intellectual hustle in which left-wing intellectuals … hold that there is no such thing as capital-T 'Truth.' There are only lower-case 'truths.' Our traditional understandings of right and wrong, true and false, are really just ways … to keep the Coalition of the Oppressed in their place.… And so the PoMos [postmodern] seek to tear down everything that 'privileges' the powerful over the powerless and to replace it with new truths more to their liking.… [Postmodernism] claims to liberate society from fixed meanings and rigid categories."[2]

"As the nineteenth-century German philosopher Friedrich Nietzsche wrote in *The Will to Power*, 'There are no facts, only interpretations.' Anyone claiming to know 'the truth' is trying to control others;

---
1 "Postmodernism," United Church of God, http://1ref.us/39.
2 Goldberg, "Obama, the Postmodernist," *USA Today*, August 5, 2008.

he is seeking power over other people."[3] The pluralistic society rides on the premise that if humans create all truth, and the Bible declares that all humans are created equal by the Creator, then all viewpoints are equally true.[4]

A good number of observers are reluctant and less sanguine in accepting that all truth is created by human design. Love God supremely and love your neighbor as yourself is the ultimate reality of life. In the postmodern worldview, religion is viewed as a cultural vehicle that transports one to the discovery of such a reality. Postmodern individuals are uncomfortable when the focus is on the transport vehicle, rather than the final destination. Philosophically, postmodernism embraces a "cafeteria religion," meaning "that a person's religion is composed of beliefs selected from different religions. For example, a person may believe in reincarnation, genuflect before a crucifix, read the Koran, and dance to honor the Great Spirit, all the while not being bothered by the fact [that] those religions, from which those varying practices originate, conflict with one another."[5] When all is said and done, all the above religious adherents are worshipping the same God.

"Postmodernism has led to multiculturalism (the belief that no culture is better than another)."[6] More often than not, the differences between religions are cultural rather than doctrinal. The manner in which Orientals and Westerners pay respect to their deceased loved ones reinforces this idea. The Chinese do so with a bowl of rice; a Westerner places a bouquet of roses at the gravesite. When will the Chinese deceased loved one get up and eat the rice in the bowl? The same time the Westerner's deceased loved one gets up and smells the fragrance of the roses. Both individuals who are buried in the ground are dead and are unaware of their loved ones efforts to remember them.

Current research on postmodernism reveals that the threefold conglomeration of secularism, pluralism, and privatism has created the perfect spiritual storm for the millennial society. Postmodernity combines "the old and the new." Not in an attempt to produce a "wonderful blend," but rather in a playful irony that tends to flatten the chain of command, undermine power structures, and invent new realities. Unlike modernity, postmodernity rejects the integrity of a single style.[7] However, the advocates of pluralism have the tendency to display a narrow-minded bias toward those who are oppositional. According to Duffy Robbins, pluralism hinges on "tolerate everything except intolerance. Every opinion is equally valid except for the opinion that every opinion is not equally valid."[8] As a result, the adherents of pluralism end up believing anything and everything.[9] Michael Polanyi, a Hungarian chemist, economist, and philosopher, made this observation about pluralism: "Its incandescence has fed on the combustion of the Christian heritage in the oxygen of Greek rationalism, and when the fuel was exhausted, the critical framework burned away."[10]

---

3   "Postmodernism," United Church of God, http://1ref.us/39.
4   Robbins, *This Way to Youth Ministry: An Introduction to the Adventure*, p. 300.
5   "Postmodernism," United Church of God, http://1ref.us/39.
6   Ibid.
7   Smith, *The End of the World As We Know It*, p. 46.
8   Wolfe, *One Nation After All*, p. 54.
9   Robbins, *This Way to Youth Ministry: An Introduction to the Adventure*, p. 298.
10 Akkerman, "The Graphic Gospel: Preaching in a Postliterate Age," Abstract, p. 22.

It is a fatal mistake to label postmodernism as an irrational philosophical meandering ideology. In his book *Deliver Us From Evil*, Ravi Zacharias frames the postmodern landscape in consequential terms, observing that one of the first causalities of pluralism is disdain for shame. Why should anybody be ashamed if there is no law, no right and wrong?[11] This question coincides with an "eleventh commandment" that our society has adopted: "Thou shall not judge."[12]

Postmodernism is at variance with the dynamos of capitalism that success and self-worth in life are measured by the standard of consumption. It also rejects the idea that a reduced faction of the populace should manipulate an economic industry that is motored by the vast majority of the working class. Postmodernism claims that the abuses of capitalism could only be solved through a revision of the "core values that inform many religious and secular communities. You could summarize them in the words of the Golden Rule: Do to others what you would want them to do to you; or, put even more simply, treat others the way you'd like to be treated (Matthew 7:12, paraphrased)."[13]

Youth and Postmodernism

Dee Hock, founder of VISA Inc., lends this succinct contribution to our discussion: "We are at that very point in time when a 400-year-old age is dying and another is struggling to be born—a shifting of culture, science, society, and institutions enormously greater than the world has ever experienced."[14]

Demographers and statisticians are predicting that by the year 2015 Generation Y (otherwise known as the Millennial Generation) will make up one-third of the U.S. population. In 2012 there were approximately forty-six million young voters between ages 18 and 29. It is of noticeable importance that "39% of Millennials identify [themselves] as non-white, making them the most diverse generation in American history."[15]

The postmodern generation born after 1980 has swiftly become the international voice in the debate of the destiny of the church, the nation, and the world. The landscape of the twenty-first century is theirs to shape. The attitude, viewpoints, and openness to change of the next generation of young people was a determining factor in both of Barack Obama's historic political victories. His political agenda sits well with the postmodern worldview. Young Americans can finally shake off their reputation for civic apathy. The youth of America elected and re-elected the forty-fourth president of the United States.

Impotence of the Individual

The chaos theory claims that tiny changes in initial conditions acting in concert can lead to major differences in outcomes. Even though the flapping of the wings of all the butterflies in San Antonio could not start a tornado in Dallas, there is a great advantage when individuals act in concert. Therefore, it is

---

11   Robbins, *This Way to Youth Ministry: An Introduction to the Adventure*, p. 303.
12   Ibid., p. 299.
13   Meakin, "The Achilles' Heel of Capitalism," *Vision*, http://1ref.us/s.
14   "Intelligence Quotes," DecentQuotes.com, http://1ref.us/2o.
15   "Youth Voting Stats," Young Democrats of America, http://1ref.us/3z.

beyond dispute that effective and lasting change could result if the working class were to join together and state their case. Those in power constantly seek to teach the opposite, saying that change comes from the wealthy and powerful or perhaps from lone inspiring individuals. They tell us that Lincoln freed the slaves; Martin Luther King brought us civil rights; and Barack Obama brought change to Washington. These are myths designed to sabotage the population so that the elite can continue to run the show. The president of the United States can only bring miniscule change to a Washington where Congress is held hostage by political dogmas that favor the elite few.

Individuals Acting in Concert

Twentieth century anthropologist Margaret Mead admonishes to "never underestimate the power of a few committed people to change the world. Indeed, it is the only thing that ever has."[16] The pages of history are full of heroes who created for themselves roles of glorious valor that they played at decisive moments in history. Even though it is the individual who has the final word in matters of morality, no single individual can alter the course of history. This awesome task is tailor-made for a cohesive group of people. Like a category four hurricane that unleashes its fury on land, the working class and the consumers have the power to stop capitalism in its tracks and force corporate icons to sit with them around the board room to discuss the state of affairs. The power is in the hands of the working class. There is no need to acquiesce to capitalism and play the game according to the rules of the elite few. The capitalist class is more beholding to the working class, for the working class is not only players in the game—they own the game. Therefore, they must be involved in setting the rules of the game.

Those who contend that the working class is no match for the megalomaniacal forces of corporate capitalism need to take a hard look at the Montgomery Bus Boycott and the Jim Crow segregation laws of the 1960s. This civil rights movement is a stubborn reminder that "little people" can triumph over the seemingly insurmountable oppositional forces. The supremacy of local patriotism over the flimsy ideals of capitalism goes unchallenged and undisputed. Unlike the capitalist class, minimum wage workers pump any extra money they make from increased wages back into local businesses and the economy through increased spending. The point is that it is social, economic, and political suicide to underestimate the power of the grass roots level of any constituency.

Common people fought in the American Revolution to liberate the thirteen colonies of North America from the British Empire. It was ordinary people horrified by slavery who worked for decades to see it abolished. It took average men and women to band together to win the right to vote. Common workers organized themselves into unions for better wages. Millions of African-Americans marched and staged boycotts to make segregation a thing of the past.[17] For the last two decades everyday people all around the world have taken large and small actions to draw the world's attention to the grave threat of global warming. Change comes from the bottom up. It has always been that way. Large broad-based grass-roots social movements are empowered by those who have faced injustice in their lives. By organizing

---

16   "Inspiration," Project True, http://1ref.us/2n.
17   Knight, "Part 3: Why Is It Breaking Down?" End of Capitalism, http://1ref.us/2v.

with neighbors, coworkers, students, family members, and friends, the working class is fighting back. The power structure of the elite few is no match for the common people working in concert.

"The centralizing of wealth and power; the vast combinations for the enrichment of the few at the expense of the many; the combinations of the poorer classes for the defense of their interests and claims; the spirit of unrest, of riot and bloodshed; the world-wide dissemination of the same teachings that led to the French Revolution—all are tending to involve the whole world in a struggle similar to that which convulsed France."[18]

Economic exploitation of peasants and the proletariat is triggering the tide of revolt against global capitalism. More and more people are on the rampage in the major cities of the world. No sooner is the dust settled on one revolt than similarly formidable social uprising rocks capitalism. The Arab Spring has resulted in revolutionary demonstrations and protests throughout the Arab world since December 2010. There have been revolutions in Tunisia and Egypt. There has been a civil war in Libya and civil uprisings in Bahrain, Syria, and Yemen. There have also been major protests in Algeria, Iraq, Jordan, and Morocco.[19]

The West is not off the hook. On March 26, 2011, more than 250,000 people attended a rally to protest against cuts in public spending in England.[20] Now consider what is happening in the United States. Occupy Wall Street has been a power to contend with. Superficially, these peaceful protests constitute the pinnacle of the millenarian clash between the capitalist and working classes.

Making use of the Internet, millions of Americans and other global citizens are expressing their dissatisfaction with the empty promises of a system that hardly ever delivers. These global strikes, protests, and revolts are misguided responses to capitalism's arrogant and self-serving policies. There are those who advocate that privatization of the public sector is the path that leads to economic success. Let them go to Bolivia and explain why the local citizens, in a united effort, elected Evo Morales its first-ever indigenous president. They elected Morales in rebellion against the privatization of the social services imposed by neo-liberalism. For example, the World Bank was responsible for the public water system, and before long the price of tap water tripled. If the skyrocketing prices were not enough, the citizens of Bolivia were also denied the privilege of collecting rainwater—it became illegal to do so. In the face of these governmental decisions, the people united and elected Morales.[21]

With increasing frequency, the global community is coming together in movements to undermine global imperialism. They are tired of a system that profits disproportionately off their labor and resources. In addition to groups of people coming together, the church can make a difference and speak out against blatant displays of abuse and misuse of the working class. I believe that when individuals and churches start denouncing the practices of corporate America people will take stock of the situation and begin listening.

---

18 White, *Education*, p. 228.
19 "Arab Spring," Wikipedia, http://1ref.us/1y.
20 "2011 London Anti-cuts Protest," Wikipedia, http://1ref.us/1q.
21 Knight, "Part 3: Why Is It Breaking Down?" End of Capitalism, http://1ref.us/2v.

Chapter 11

The Economic Utopia

Overview

A lasting solution to the economic crisis may arise from a combination of what is good from both socialism and capitalism. This will require change across the spectrum. In transparent fashions, this chapter allows all to see the beauty of perhaps the most equitable compensation system in the world.

The Cause of the Economic Downturn

The position of certain economists is that whatever or whosoever was responsible for the financial crisis should fix it. The most recent recession in the United States is perhaps the most devastating. Unlike the Great Depression of the 1930s, the United States is dealing with three wars, as well as Iran and North Korea's quest to acquire nuclear weapons. Contrary to conventional wisdom, faulty loans and deregulation are not the greatest contributing factors to the bad economy. Some financial technocrats trace the root cause of the notorious volatility and downturn of the United States economy to a financial crisis. Here is the genius of American politics. Not only is this a distraction from identifying whom the real culprits are, but it also provides the opportunity to satiate political "thirst" by drinking from the bitter "cup" of blame. Pointing the condemning finger of blame merely passes on the legacy of failure to future generations. The recent economic recession is made up of a lot of little pieces, such as executive pay, which has been outrageous since 1983, and greed. However, suggesting that these are the only factors involved overlooks the imperial impetus hidden in the background. This is a crisis that affects all the parts of the system. Manufacturing, services, and finances are included, but in no way restricted. It did not begin with finance, and it will not end with finance.[1]

---

1   Wolff, "Capitalism Hits the Fan," http://1ref.us/3x.

From 1820 to 1970 productivity and wages went up simultaneously. Corporations enjoyed rising profit while the working class enjoyed rising wages. Federal minimum wages rose steadily from $0.75 in 1955 to $2.90 in 1979.[2] It is clearly seen why this was the era when American prestige reached its peak. Put yourself in the shoes of the American society during the time in question. With the glories of 150 years of prosperity still fresh in their mind, the American family embarked on a spending spree. The working class believed that if they were doing well, then their children would do even better. It was not long after this that American society began to define its self-worth and measure its success in life by the standards of consumption. Americans became wedded to consumption in ways that other working classes in the world had not and perhaps still have not done. Before long the advertising industry was introduced, which forever bonded American society with the passion for consumption.[3]

Flattened Wages and Rising Profits

In 1970 there was a dramatic change in America among the working class. The symbiotic relationship between the capitalist and the working classes was replaced by a capitalism that systematically pillaged, plundered, and exploited the poor and working classes. Wages were flattened and even started to slightly plummet, and health coverage was no longer a right but a privilege. All the while consumption continued to rise, and businesses enjoyed more and more profit. Minimum wages were flattened at $3.35 from 1981 to 1989. Then, in 1991 it rose to $4.25, where it remained frozen until 1996. It rose to $5.15 in 1997, but it remained at that rate for almost ten years, from 1997 to 2006.[4]

Most economists trace the beginning of the recent recession back to 2001. Connect the dots, and the inevitable conclusion is that rising productivity, in contrast to decreasing wages, was what started producing huge profits for the capitalist corporations and sparked the recession. The only solution lies in increasing minimum wage to a living wage.

Economical Crossroads for the Working Class

The American working class came to an economical crossroad and was faced with a serious dilemma. There was no rising wages for a population determined to measure success by the amount of consumption it could afford. The average American took second and third jobs to help make ends meet and sustain their lifestyle. American families began working themselves to exhaustion to keep up with an expected standard of living. However, this resulted in increased expenses the likes of a second car, work clothes, child care, etc. Families began to be torn apart by the increased workload, and the added stress and tension resulted in the need for counseling and therapy, which was an additional expense. Divorce and drug consumption escalated. Thus, the extra income from extra jobs was neutralized by the extra costs associated with taking the additional job.

---

2 "Federal Minimum Wages Rate, 1955–2013," Infoplease, http://1ref.us/2d.
3 Wolff, "Capitalism Hits the Fan," http://1ref.us/3x.
4 "Federal Minimum Wages Rate, 1955–2013," Infoplease, http://1ref.us/2d.

The working class had no alternative but to embark on a barrowing spree to keep up with their consumption. As businesses continued experiencing increasing profits from rising productivity and flattened wages, the working class was haunted by the memories of unbridled consumption. Corporate America seized the moment and moved in for the kill, capitalizing on the inability of the working class to increase consumption. To increase consumption, they made funds available to the proletariat to do so. The new motto became, "When you cannot earn the money to buy it, you can borrow it."

The genius of capitalism is that instead of increasing wages, corporations lent money to the working class to get them to consume more. They then turned around and charged inflated interest stipulated by the credit score from the credit bureaus. This entire system was monopolized by the very same economic industry. This resulted in the American working class, who became excellent borrowers, to be heavily indebted to the capitalists. This triggered off a new round of horrendous exploitation of the working class by the capitalist elites.[5]

One may wonder how the government could just stand by and watch this happen, but the reality is that the government endorsed this crime against its citizens.

The Erosion of Family Values

Capitalism rose to the pinnacle of prosperity in the United States during the 1980s.[6] Productivity was on the rise, and wages were flattened. Businesses made huge profits on the interest that households were paying to borrow money, and the working class continued consuming even more. All the while, nobody was paying attention to the irreparable damage to the family aggravated by these psychological pressures.[7]

It was at this point that the political perpetrators made their dramatic entrance. Focusing on family values, they cunningly found a way to stay in power by positioning themselves as champions of the families who were falling apart. They vowed to protect the American family against the very consequences of what they had invoked in the first place. The perpetrators of the crime are now claiming to be the prosecutor, which is a great strategy. They orchestrated the changes that collapsed the family, presented themselves as the champions of family values, then turned around and threw the bulk of the blame on their opponents. The decline of the American family was not catalyzed by a liberal agenda. It was triggered by the abuses of capitalism and championed by politicians who favored the rich.

The working class is unable to sustain themselves or their families. They must sell their time and energy for a *wage* to survive. "People are then squeezed dry by the system and made to work harder and longer, but always for less. They do not see the profits their work produces, because those profits are invested by their bosses to acquire yet more capital, and make yet more profits."[8] The cycle never ends.

---

5   Wolff, "Capitalism Hits the Fan," http://1ref.us/3x.
6   Goolsbee, "Democratizing Capitalism," *Blueprint Magazine*, July 22, 2006.
7   "Capitalism Destroys the Family, Admits BUSINESS WEEK Magazine," reprinted from *The People* March 25, 1995, http://1ref.us/26.
8   "Who Is the Real Capitalism?" Waspadafurqon's Blog, http://1ref.us/3v.

Exhausted and anxiety ridden, the working class is now buried alive under mountains of unsustainable debts they cannot repay. People borrowed money they couldn't pay back. The working class started walking away from their obligations by the millions. Capitalism was hit where it is most vulnerable. Consumers stopped buying. Suddenly, "*risks* to investors become intolerable. Values crash, loans cease, the markets freeze, ships remain in the docks, factories halt, workers lose their jobs, and the media tries to keep a smiling face while delivering the [grim] news."[9] Nobody was prepared for this and the entire economical system collapsed. A recession was born. Here is how Steven Orchard assesses the situation:

> But if there's one truth that emerges from this economic carnage, it is that "irrational exuberance" is costly; temperance and prudence in the recent boom would have been a desirable alternative. Why then, would we not apply that same lesson to the bust?
>
> Our current financial crisis was created by greed—in overreaching home buyers and insatiable bankers alike. All enjoyed the benefits of hyper-liquidity. The bubble grew incrementally, and none of us wanted it to contract. Like frogs in a warming pot, we collectively failed to recognize an overheating economy in the form of unsustainable expansion.[10]

It is undisputed that both Main Street and Wall Street always light the fire of a recession. When the facts are accessed and analyzed, justice rules in favor of Main Street. A desperate working class grabbed at the "straw" of predatory loans thrown down to them by Wall Street and tried to pull themselves out in an effort to make things work with their flattened wages. However, in the midst of trying to better themselves, they were lectured from both sides about how they had no business taking out loans they could not afford. And somehow the blame for the recession fell on the working class.

American People Speaking in Paradoxes

It is obvious that neither communism nor capitalism holds the answer to a broken global economy. According to an Eastern European proverb, "Capitalism is man exploiting man; communism is just the opposite."[11] In the old Soviet Union, capitalism triumphed over communism. In America, capitalism triumphed over democracy. As it stands now, capitalism is everything *except* a democracy. It is dressed like a democracy, looks like a democracy, smells like a democracy, and even taste like a democracy. However, in reality it is a dictatorship monopolized by the elite few.

Communism passed away two decades ago, and I predict that capitalism is soon to follow. More and more Americans are rejecting the abuses of capitalism and are gravitating toward a democratized capitalism. This seems to be the only economic industry that can win back the trust of the American

---
9   Ibid.
10 Orchard, "Who Crippled Capitalism?" *Vision*, http://1ref.us/40.
11 "Eastern Europe Proverb Quotes," Thinkexist.com, http://1ref.us/2b.

people. They are growing more sympathetic toward a kind of socialism in which government, working class, and democratized enterprises are proactive in providing equal proportional benefits to all entities. America clamors for a hybrid system that draws from the noble principles that constitute the best of both capitalism and socialism. In this system, the government levels the playing field, and it is no longer who has what, but who gets what.

Martin Luther King Jr. said, "Communism forgets that life is individual. Capitalism forgets that life is social, and the kingdom of brotherhood is found neither in the thesis of communism nor [in] the antithesis of capitalism but in a higher synthesis. It is found in a higher synthesis that combines the truths of both."[12]

If you poll Americans regarding this issue, contradicting results emerge. Americans are tired of the abuses of capitalism, but they want no part of the dictates of big government and socialism. The American vernacular demands an economic system that updates the regulatory structure with sound rules that reward drive and innovation. The system Americans seek should increase the minimum wage to a living wage instead of increasing the profits and assets of the rich. It would appear that the American people fully understand the importance of the consumer's role in the formation of wealth and that is why their message through the polls is clear. They want a government that rises above the interests of only one class and invests more in the middle class. This will make businesses more competitive in areas like health care, energy, and education.

In the movie *Capitalism: A Love Story*, Michael Moore proposed democratized capitalism as an alternative to traditional capitalism. This system would allow "average folks to have a say in how their money is used, from the workplace on up to the government. Moore takes us inside co-ops in America where workers vote on decisions about finances democratically, and where salaries are equal and adequate for everyone in the company. In one factory, the assembly line workers and the CEO each make about $60,000 annually."[13]

The Seventh-day Adventist church organization, in which I am a practicing ordained minister, offers a similar compensation plan to what Moore is proposing. Ministers, teachers, and administrators are paid from the tithes and offerings that the church collects. Their salary is based on regional differences and the cost of living of the area. The pay scale for the church has a narrow band with only a 12 percent differential between an ordained minister and the General Conference president, the highest position in the church.[14]

The recent global recession that was conceived in the economic womb of flattened wages has been growing for centuries. It has reached a climax in our own times. The recession will come to a grinding halt when the working class becomes the recipients of living wages, which will empower them to return to former consumption practices. This was what it was before the 1970s when the working class was the recipient of living wages.

---

12 "Martin Luther King Jr. Quotes," Goodreads, http://1ref.us/34.
13 Knight, "Anti-Capitalism Goes Mainstream: Review of 'Capitalism: A Love Story,' " End of Capitalism, http://1ref.us/2t.
14 "NAD Remuneration Scales for January 1, 2005," Seventh-day Adventist Church, http://1ref.us/37.

Today, there is a widening gap between the delusions of such past utopia and the eccentric forces of entrenched greed and skullduggery. Notwithstanding, perhaps the preamble to its ceremonial burying is now in the process of being written. Martin Luther King Jr. said, "When years have rolled past and when the blazing light of truth is focused on this marvelous age in which we live, men and women will know and children will be taught that we have a finer land, a better people, a more noble civilization because these humble children of God were willing to suffer for righteousness' sake."[15]

On that day all of God's children—democrats, republicans, socialists, capitalists, the working class, imperialists, totalitarians, Jews, Gentiles, Catholics, Protestants, Hindus, Muslims, rich, and poor—will sit down around one great table of the brotherhood of humanity and tell their children how the entire globe was liberated from the manacles of capitalism's greed. Then will come to pass the words of the late President Ronald Reagan, in his farewell address to America on January 11, 1989: "I've spoken of the shining city all my political life, but I don't know if I ever quite communicated what I saw when I said it. But in my mind it was a tall proud city built on rocks stronger than oceans, wind-swept, God-blessed, and teeming with people of all kinds living in harmony and peace, a city with free ports that hummed with commerce and creativity, and if there had to be city walls, the walls had doors and the doors were open to anyone with the will and the heart to get here."[16]

---

[15] "Acceptance Speech at Nobel Peace Prize Ceremony," The Martin Luther King, Jr. Research and Education Institute, http://1ref.us/1s.

[16] "Ronald Reagan Quotes," NotableQuotes, http://1ref.us/3f.

Chapter 12

Religious-Political Issues

Overview

Through a series of groundbreaking revelations, religious-political issues—the likes of same-sex marriages and abortion—are confronted in ways never done before. Same-sex marriage is a felony and condemned on the basis that homosexuality is condemned in the Bible. Within this chapter I will discuss why eating shellfish, committing adultery, etc., should share the same fate. This chapter also addresses the two sides of the abortion debate. This chapter asks tough questions, but it also provides some honest answers.

The United States of Religions

Christianity overwhelmingly shapes the religious landscape in North America. It is estimated that three in four adults identify themselves as Christians. Nevertheless, America was not founded only on Christian values. It was founded on values that allowed its citizens to practice any religion based on the free dictates of their conscience. Seventy-three percent of Americans claim they are Christians. "According to a 2002 survey by the Pew forum, nearly 6 in 10 Americans said that religion plays an important role in their lives."[1]

Because religious adherents make up a huge chunk of the United States population, politicians cannot afford the luxury of shying away from religious-political issues. Religious and cultural baggage forms a unique blend in the lives of most Americans. This is often what drives their beliefs and their values. If politicians truly hope to speak to people where they are at, and communicate hopes and values in a way that is relevant, the field of religious discourse cannot be abandoned.

---

1   "Religion in the United States," Wikipedia, http://1ref.us/3e.

Religious-Political Gap

Making the connection between religion and politics is not only dangerous, but it is tricky. In the arena of religious-political issues, socialism, without the benefit of a trial, is condemned as inefficient and corrupt. Secularism is equated with atheism, and sensitive domestic policies can effortlessly be branded as dictatorial. In the religious-political world, there is a thin line between heresy and prophecy. The social issues addressed in this chapter are presented in a scholarly, responsible, and well-informed manner.

Following is an excerpt from a speech that Senator Barack Obama gave in 2006:

> The political divide in this country has fallen sharply along religious lines. Indeed, the single biggest 'gap' in party affiliation among white Americans today is not between men and women, or those who reside in so-called Red States and those who reside in Blue, but between those who attend church regularly and those who don't.[2]

Politicians from both sides of the aisle make their greatest blunder when they think that religious Americans care only about issues such as abortion and gay marriage, school prayer, and intelligent design. While it is true that they do care about these issues, it is a myth that they are not deeply concerned about socio-religious political issues the likes of same-sex marriages, the Arab-Israeli conflict, health care, immigration, Wall Street, unemployment benefits, minimum wage, welfare, social security, and the environment. These issues are also important to Christians.

It is so tempting to hide behind a constitution that was intended to protect a local Baptist community in Danbury, Connecticut, from encroachments of the state against that particular church. The metaphoric wall of separation "was used exclusively [by President Thomas Jefferson] to keep the state out of the church's business, not to keep the church out of the state's business."[3] Politicians claim that regardless of one's personal beliefs, constitutional principles have their hands tied tightly. Therefore, the discussion of religion in the public square is considered to be off limits and intolerant. The highways of American history are littered with the wreckage from the head on collision between the distortions of the separation of church and state. Why should the church be asked to vote on socio-religious political issues, but by the same token public discussion of said issues is off limits? What is the difference between a public vote and a public discussion? Why can politicians campaign in churches to get elected but, as soon as they are elected, they remember that there is a separation of church and state?

While politicians continue hiding behind a ghost wall of a misapplied constitutional principle, it is becoming more obvious that the road to success in American politics winds through socio-religious political territories. The individual who wins the debate on these issues will win elections. It is political suicide to backpedal and avoid the conversation about religious values altogether, fearful of offending

---

2   White, "Barack Obama's Controversial '06 Speech on Religion & Politics," About.com US Liberal Politics, http://1ref.us/3u.

3   "Separation of Church and State - The Metaphor and the Constitution," AllAboutHistory.org, http://1ref.us/3i.

religious adherents. Politicians, lawmakers, and world leaders make their greatest blunder leaving God out of the mix as they grapple with these socio-religious political issues. We are reaping a harvest of calamity, all of which stems from the love of money, which is the root of all evil (1 Tim. 6:10). Loving God and others is the solution. Putting this fundamental creed into practice would end the exploitation of the poor by the rich, halt all environmental abuses, lead to a deeper respect for other religions, solve the Arab-Israeli conflict, better our economy, solve the abortion crisis, and end legalizing same-sex marriages. During the last two presidential elections of 2008 and 2012, the victor won the debate on almost all the previously mentioned socio-religious political issues.

Same-sex Marriage

The gay community is growing, and the social attitude toward homosexuality is changing. In 2013 Pew Global Research found that 51 to 60 percent of Americans feel that society should accept homosexuality.[4] It is understandable why politicians handle this issue with care, because the gay community and those who support homosexuality can sway the outcome of any election. Some states are going beyond simply accepting a homosexual lifestyle and are now legalizing same-sex marriage.

Those who oppose same-sex marriage usually argue that homosexuality is condemned in the Bible (see Gen. 19:1–11; Lev. 18:22; 1 Cor. 6:9, 10; Rom. 1:26, 27; and Rev. 22:15). If we examine homosexuality in the Bible, we see that it arose within the Jewish nation when the Israelites incorporated Baal worship into their lives alongside their worship of Yahweh. "They had one God for crises and another god for everyday life. The actual worship of Ba'al was carried out in terms of imitative magic whereby sexual acts by both male and female temple prostitutes were understood to arouse Ba'al who then brought rain to make Mother Earth fertile."[5] It is easily deduced that at times there were more male or female prostitutes. The overflow group would form themselves into gay and lesbians pairs. God created Adam and Eve, not Adam and Steve.

The legal system in the United States evolved out of biblical laws, and the Bible condemns homosexual behavior. Therefore, some argue that same-sex marriage should be illegal and banned in the United States. I am in accord that there is zero support for homosexuality and same-sex marriage in the Bible. However, where do we draw the line in relation to government's involvement in the lives of the American people?

Adultery is one of the ten commandments. Should every adulterer be prosecuted by the government for breaking a biblical law? If this were the case, the jail population of almost every nation would outnumber its free citizens! What about the passages in Leviticus 11 and Deuteronomy 14 that condemn the consumption of swine and shellfish, calling it an abomination? Should eating these unclean foods be considered a criminal act? Should these biblical guidelines be legal issues? No.

I propose that same-sex marriage should not be a legal issue. God created us with the power of choice. We are free to exercise that choice, even when it goes against God's will. Gays and lesbians have

---
4 "Homosexuality," Wikipedia, http://1ref.us/2l (accessed April 3, 2014).
5 Bratcher, "Ba'al Worship in the Old Testament," The Voice, Christian Resource Institute, http://1ref.us/24.

the same power to choose whether they want to follow God's Word and His ways as much I have the power to choose to follow God. God is the one we all have to answer to in the end.

Consider this: Of the ten commandments recorded in Exodus 20, only three are considered as legal infringements of the U.S. Constitution: you shall not bear false witness against your neighbor, you shall not steal, and you shall not commit murder. As the end of the world draws near, another commandment will become a legal issue. The fourth commandment, which addresses the worship of God on the seventh day of the week, will be brought into scrutiny. (See chapter 14 for more on this topic.)

It seems fairly obvious why our nation's legal system does not focus on adding more biblical commandments to the law books. Violations of the other commandments are more subjective and difficult to prosecute in a court of law. The ones that have legal repercussions are measurable. Fingerprints can be found on the stolen goods. DNA can lead to the conviction of the perpetrator of a murder. And a person bearing false witness can be exposed by a lie detector machine.

Now back to the issue at hand. I feel that it would be just as inhumane to throw somebody in jail for their choice to eat a piece of hog meat, as it would be for somebody's choice to marry someone of the same-sex. Both actions are condemned in the Bible. From the foundation of the world, God gave His creatures the greatest power in the universe—the power of choice. People are free to even choose a lifestyle that goes against what He desires for them. People are free to engage in same-sex marriages or to eat all manner of unclean foods. That is humanity's God-given choice, but God will judge people based on their actions and decisions on this earth (Eccl. 11:9). I believe that in God's eyes morality is not legislated—it is done by choice and not forced.

The Lesbian, Gay, Bisexual, and Transgender Community

The lesbian, gay, bisexual, and transgender (LGBT) community has harnessed universal acceptance, and this lifestyle is no longer viewed by the world as sinful. But make no mistake, the goal of the LGBT community is to get the church on board, which means that the church would not consider this lifestyle as sinful. The strategy employed by the allies of the gay community is the same the devil used on Eve. She was engaged in a conversation, and she ended up believing a lie: "Ye shall not surely die" (Gen. 3:4, KJV).

The church makes its greatest blunder when it engages in public discussion and debate on the subject of gay relationships. This is when the body of Christ rides the peak of its vulnerability. It is the intention of the allies of the gay community to engage the global community in conversation on this sensitive subject in order to convince people that gay relationships are not sinful. The strategy is working to perfection.

But there is an unfounded accusation that the church is hostile toward the gay community and that this community is the most ostracized of all sinners. If there is any hostility at all, it stems from the resentment of being pressured by the allies of the gay community to embrace the gay community just as they are. Acceptance means that the church should be comfortable with their lifestyle and in turn should extend to them the opportunity to serve in leadership roles just as they are. But this would result in loving the sinner and the sin, instead of loving the sinner and hating the sin.

In their quest to push back on this, the church has taken the fight to another level—discrimination. When you deny people an active place in society based on their sexual orientation, you have reached the next stop—the twilight zone. Isn't it the same benevolent God who sends the rain on the just and the unjust? There is a thin line between freedom of decision and the imprisoning walls of discrimination. The definition of morality is guilt before an action, and in a world governed by choice, this cannot be legislated.

It would do us well to be reminded that the church falls short when the message of Jesus is softened or tweaked in the name of culture and popular beliefs, not just in regards to the issue of homosexuality. When church leaders overlook the raging idols of this age such as money, sex, immorality, and power, the cost of Christianity disappears. Christianity without a cost is Christianity without the cross. And what is Christianity without the cross? It is a sad day when a church becomes a mirror that reflects our particular preferences, desires, and dreams. The firm conviction of some is that it is the church that shapes and changes our preferences, desires, and dreams.

Embracing people when the moral impact of their lives is impeccable is an enticing commodity. However, embracing them when they are in the gutters of the promiscuous niches of postmodernism is another matter. But there is no depth in sin to which a sinner can sink where the love of God cannot reach them. A good strategy for the church is to first open its heart wide and love the gay community as Jesus loved them. It is only then that the human clay would be ready to be shaped by the Divine Potter and restored into His image.

Abortion

In dealing with the question of abortion, great care should be exercised. Its legality or illegality depends on whether a life is taken or not taken in the process or whether the zygote is a living human or not. The abortion question is fundamentally not about a parent's rights, but rather about when life begins. Taking the cue from Jeremiah, many believe that life begins at conception: "Before I formed you in the womb I knew you; before you were born I sanctified you; I ordained you a prophet to the nations" (Jer. 1:5). Note that before Jeremiah was born, God knew him, He sanctified him, and He ordained him. Jeremiah was a human being in his mother's womb.

The presence of the complete number of chromosomes in the zygote is strong scientific evidence that life begins at conception. If life indeed begins at conception, then we need to put a system in place that will discourage pregnancy being viewed as a disease and abortion as the cure. But by the same token, this same system should make exceptions for situations where a thirteen-year-old girl becomes pregnant from rape or incest, the fetus is immensely deformed with no chance of survival, or the choice must be made to save the mother or the unborn child.

Six Cities of Refuge

Here is a suggestion of how the issue of justified and unjustified abortions could be handled. This is a religious-political discussion. Therefore, the Bible should speak. In Numbers 35 we find detailed instructions concerning what should be done if someone kills someone accidentally or unintentionally. The law was clear and unequivocal. If a human being was intentionally murdered, the murderer would be judged and immediately put to death. Unintentional and self-defense killings were dealt with differently.

There were six cities of refuge, three on both sides of the Jordan River. If an individual was accidentally or unintentionally killed, the killer was not automatically executed. Notwithstanding, he or she had to flee to the nearest city of refuge to await judgment and possible vindication. It is of noticeable importance that whether a life was taken in self-defense or was accidental, the perpetrator was under the condemnation of the law until vindication came. Even after the vindication came, the individual had to remain within the confines of the biblical penitentiary until the death of the high priest (Num. 35:25).

This system underscores that God, the Creator of life, is offended when a life is taken, be it accidental, unintentional, or in self-defense.

Every case of abortion should be handled under the umbrella of the "city of refuge" mentality. All abortions, justified or unjustified, are the taking of innocent lives and should at all times be judged under the condemnation of the law. The unjustified cases should be dealt with severely. Both the mother and the attending physician should be judged accordingly in a court of law. If convicted they should be persecuted according to the demands of the laws that are applicable. The justified cases—pregnancies caused by incest or rape, a severely deformed fetus with no chance of survival, or a pregnancy that endangers the health or life of the mother— should be handled by certified medical personnel.

Those who oppose the pro-choice position argue that it opens the floodgates of promiscuousness. In the pro-choice position, pregnancy is considered a disease and abortion the cure. From this perspective, abortion becomes the lubrication for a grim political killing machine responsible for the murdering of millions of innocent lives every year. All this is carried on under the umbrella of birth control. The "city of refuge" mentality advocates that no other abortion should be funded with any category of funding. The primary reason why many use abortion as birth control is because they know they can. This approach will not stop every abortion used for birth control, but the number of abortions for such dark purposes will be reduced considerably.

The battle over health care reform has placed pro-life advocates between a rock and a hard place. On one hand, they insist in enacting laws that allow thousands of fellow Americans (children, youth, and adults) to die annually because they have no health insurance. Yet, with the same stroke of the brush, pro-life advocates contend that there is no excuse whatsoever for willfully taking the life of an innocent human being—a fetus. Isn't the life of a child, teenager, adult, or elderly person just as valuable as an unborn child?

In the other corner, there are those who advocate that a woman's right to choose justifies the taking of a life as birth control. If this holds true, then an African American man could exercise the power of choice to murder a Caucasian under the pretext that such an act is to control white supremacy. Could such a course of action ever be upheld in a court of law? The same principle should be applied when abortion is used as birth control. These tough questions find answers in neither the thesis of the pro-life position, nor in the antithesis of the pro-choice position.

The answer to this difficult question may be found in a higher synthesis that combines both positions as stated by the General Conference of Seventh-day Adventists Executive Committee. This statement provides a comforting congruency between the two sides of this issue:

> The Church does not serve as conscience for individuals; however, it should provide moral guidance. Abortions for reasons of birth control, gender selection, or convenience are not condoned by the Church. Women, at times however, may face exceptional circumstances that present serious moral or medical dilemmas, such as significant threats to the pregnant woman's life, serious jeopardy to her health, severe congenital defects carefully diagnosed in the fetus, and pregnancy resulting from rape or incest. The final decision whether to terminate the pregnancy or not should be made by the pregnant woman after appropriate consultation. She should be aided in her decision by accurate information, biblical principles, and the guidance of the Holy Spirit. Moreover, these decisions are best made within the context of healthy family relationships.[6]

C. S. Lewis and others argue that "when an adult is killed, at least they had a chance to enjoy life, and perhaps they had a chance to fight back and try to defend themselves against their killer. But an unborn child is helpless to defend himself or herself. When an unborn child is killed, it is deprived even of the chance to enjoy life. For this reason, … abortion is worse than murder."[7]

---

6 "The Seventh-day Adventist Church: Its Beliefs and Practices," ReligiousTolerance.org, http://1ref.us/3j.
7 Sheedy, "The 'Pro-Life' and 'Pro-Choice' Position on Abortion," The Nolan Chart, http://1ref.us/3k.

Chapter 13

The Arab-Israeli Conflict

Overview

The focus of this chapter is on the Arab-Israeli conflict and who should take responsibility for the ignominious fiasco of the Palestinian people. Jews and Arabs literally share paternal roots with Abraham. Ownership of Palestine should not be by conquest; it belongs to whomever God promised it to. God promised the land to Abraham and to all those born in his household. Therefore, both his sons (Jews and Arabs) have legitimate rights to Palestine. This is just a preview as to why a two-state solution could put an end to this ongoing crisis. This is a biblical position. Even though Israelis, Palestinians, and neighboring Arabs are equally to be blamed for the Arab-Israeli fiasco, discover why I, in a nuanced and wide-ranging fashion, pin the bulk of the blame on Great Britain.

Background of Conflict

The Arab-Israeli conflict attests to the presence of an omnipotent God who sets up and removes kings and directs nations. The conflict between Palestinian Arabs and Jews began around the turn of the twentieth century. Some believe that the root of the conflict stems from the religious background of both groups and the quest to reside in the same territory and set up dominance in the land of Palestine,[1] while others believe that it has nothing to do with religion and everything to do with land.[2]

> Following the war, of 1948-1949, this land was divided into three parts: the state of Israel, the West Bank (of the Jordan River), and the Gaza Strip.

---

1 "Arab-Israeli Conflict," Wikipedia, http://1ref.us/1v.
2 Beinin, "Palestine, Israel and the Arab-Israeli Conflict—A Primer," Middle East Research & Information Project, http://1ref.us/21.

It is a small area—approximately 10,000 square miles, or about the size of the state of Maryland. The competing claims are not reconcilable if one group exercises exclusive political control over all of it. [The Arab-Israeli conflict has deteriorated and mushroomed into an unending explosion of violence in the region.] Jewish claims to this land are based on the biblical promise to Abraham and his descendants, on the fact that this was the historical site of the ancient Jewish kingdom of Israel and Judea, and on the Jews' need for a haven from European anti-Semitism. Palestinian Arabs claims to the land are based on their continuous residence in the country for hundreds of years and the fact that they represented the demographic majority until 1948. They reject the notion that a biblical-era kingdom constitutes the basis for a valid modern claim. If Arabs engage the biblical argument at all, they maintain that since Abraham's son Ishmael is the forefather of the Arabs, then God's promise of the land to the children of Abraham includes Arabs as well. They do not believe that they should forfeit their land to compensate Jews for Europe's crimes against Jews.[3]

Efraim Karsh, a prominent exponent of this subject, penned the following:

Since the Roman destruction of Jewish statehood in the land that has subsequently come to be known as Palestine, exile and dispersion have become the hallmark of Jewish existence. Even in its ancestral homeland the Jewish community was relegated to a small minority under a long succession of imperial occupiers—Byzantines, Arabs, Seljuk Turks, crusaders, Mamluks, and Ottoman Turks—who inflicted repression and dislocation upon Jewish life.

This forced marginalization notwithstanding, not only was the Jewish presence in Palestine never totally eliminated, but the Jews' longing for their ancestral homeland, or Zion, occupied a focal place in their collective memory for millennia and became an integral part of Jewish religious ritual.[4]

Helpful Factors to Solve the Conflict

After Israel inherited the land of Canaan, intermarriage and tolerance resulted in the Canaanites eventually integrating into the Jewish race. It is clear that Palestinians cannot claim any descent from the ancient Canaanites. If this was so, they would speak the language of the ancient Canaanites, which was Hebrew.[5] "Indeed, there is no such a [sic] thing like a Palestinian people, or a Palestinian culture, or a Palestinian language, or a Palestinian history. There has never been any Palestinian state, neither

---

3   "Primer on Palestine, Israel and the Arab-Israeli Conflict," Middle East Research and Information Project, http://1ref.us/3b.
4   Karsh, *Islamic Imperialism: A History*, p. 140.
5   "The True Identity of the So-called Palestinians," Myths, Hypotheses and Facts Concerning the Origin of Peoples, http://1ref.us/3r.

any Palestinian archaeological find nor coinage. The present-day 'Palestinians' are an Arab people, with Arab culture, Arabic language and Arab history. They have their own Arab states from where they came into the Land of Israel about one century ago to contrast the Jewish immigration."[6]

After World War I Palestine was not granted independence as other nations were. Instead, it was managed by Great Britain. The Balfour Declaration of 1917 states:

> His Majesty's Government view with favour the establishment in Palestine of a national home for the Jewish people, and will use their best endeavours to facilitate the achievement of this object, it being clearly understood that nothing shall be done which may prejudice the civil and religious rights of existing non-Jewish communities in Palestine, or the rights and political status enjoyed by Jews in any other country.[7]

A few years after the Balfour declaration (early 1920s), large numbers of Jewish people migrated to Palestine. This migration went on for years and peaked in the 1930s and 1940s. Under British rule Palestine was divided between Jordan and Israel, the larger portion given to Jordan. This was a scathing indictment of the Arab legacy and delineated the broad contours of the nascent Arab-Israeli conflict for decades to come. A bilateral dispute between Arabs and Jews in Palestine was transformed into a pan-Arab-Jewish conflict. Violence was the primary instrument used for opposing Jewish national aspirations.

At the end of World War I, Palestinian Arabs accounted for about 90 percent of the population. The insinuation that they were intruders in Palestine did not sit well with the Arabs. They were outraged at this prospect. Egyptian President Gamal Abdel Nasser felt that the Balfour Declaration was a shrewd political move by the British to divide and conquer, suppress, weaken, and destroy Arab nationalism.[8] This justifies why the Jews were the first in the line of fire. It also constitutes the core reason for the Arab rejection of the statehood of Israel.

This is why Yasser Arafat expressed himself in an interview with these words: "Our ancestors fought the crusaders for a hundred years, and later Ottoman imperialism, then British and French imperialism for years and years. It is our duty to take over the banner of struggle from them and hand it on untarnished and flying as proudly as ever to the generations that come after us. We shall never commit a crime against them, the crime of permitting the existence of a racialist state in the heart of the Arab world."[9]

"While Jewish immigration to Palestine in the 1920's caused little alarm, the situation escalated markedly with the rise of Nazi persecution in Europe. Large numbers of European Jews flocked to Palestine, inflaming nationalist passions among all Arabs, who feared the creation of a Jewish state in

---

6   Ibid.
7   "The Balfour Declaration of 1917," History Learning Site, http://1ref.us/20 (accessed January 23, 2014).
8   Karsh, *Islamic Imperialism: A History*, p. 139.
9   Ibid., p. 185.

The Arab-Israeli Conflict

which they would be the losers. Palestinian resistance erupted into a full-scale revolt which lasted from 1936–39."[10]

The ticking Palestinian time bomb started in 1937 and came to a head when disgruntled Palestinians rebelled and started demanding an independent nation. The British abandoned the territory without providing any clear boundary. The entire matter of who owned what was passed on to the United Nations, who determined that the dispute be decided through arbitration rather than by war. They proposed side-by-side Israeli and Palestinian states with Jerusalem being part of both.

The Jewish people continued to move to Israel. By 1948 demand for more space led to the occupation of three-quarters of the Palestinian state, including part of Jerusalem. This led to the 1948 Arab-Israeli War. It was during this war that parts of Palestine, namely, the West Bank and the Gaza Strip, were conquered by Jordan and Egypt. Neither country allowed Palestinian self-determination in the parts of Palestine conquered during this war.

"On April 4, 1950, the territory [West Bank] was formally annexed to Jordan, its residents became Jordanian citizens, and they were increasingly integrated into the kingdom's economic, political, and social structures. For its part, the Egyptian government showed no desire to annex the Gaza Strip ... but ruled it as an occupied military zone."[11]

"This did not imply support of Palestinian nationalism, however, or of any sort of collective political awareness among Palestinians."[12] Nasser and others contended that it was against their interests to allow statehood to the Palestinian Arabs as there was no room in the neighboring vicinity for another nation.[13]

Palestinian refugees were denied Egyptian citizenship and remained in squalid, harshly supervised camps. This was a last-ditch effort to tarnish the image of Israel in the eyes of the West and arouse pan-Arab sentiments. It was in line with Egypt's political ambitions to deny statehood to Palestinians. Palestinian refugees fleeing to Arab states were derided as a cowardly lot who had shamefully deserted their homeland while expecting others to fight for them. There were repeated calls for the return of the refugees to Palestine. At the very least, the young men of military age should return and fight. The Palestinians did not hesitate to respond in kind, blaming the Arab states, rather than Israel, for their disaster.[14]

In 1967, after an innumerable number of intermittent skirmishes, the simmering tension between Israel and pan-Arabism boiled over. Israel went to war with Egypt and Jordan. This was the famous Six-Day War. It was expected that Israel would suffer a routing defeat. Instead, within three hours of the outbreak of hostilities, Egypt's entire air force was wiped out on the ground. The 1948 war paled in comparison to the conflict in 1967, in which Israel took over all the land, including the Egyptian and Syrian territories. The war's swift and decisive nature provided a clear victor—the Israelis. When

---
10   "The Tragedy of Palestine," The Hashemite Kingdom of Jordan, http://1ref.us/3q.
11   Karsh, *Islamic Imperialism: A History*, p. 145.
12   Karsh, "What Occupation?" *Commentary*, July-August 2002.
13   Laffin, *The PLO Connections*, p. 127.
14   Karsh, *Islamic Imperialism: A History*, p. 146

the war ended, Israel had extended its control over vast Palestinian territories formerly owned by Jordan and Egypt. Israel had quadrupled its territory, which now extended from the Suez Canal, to the Jordan River, to the Golan Heights. The newly acquired territory now included the Gaza Strip, the Sinai Peninsula, the West Bank, and all of Jerusalem.[15]

Although the United Nations encouraged Israel to give back the land they acquired during the war, Israel refused. Over the years, there have been multiple attempts to bring peace to the region and settle the conflict. In 1995 and 1998, agreements were signed to allow Palestinians to settle in the West Bank. But despite these agreements, tensions still run high on both sides of the issue.[16]

Reaching a Solution

Results gleaned from researching this discussion seem to suggest that the Palestinian Arabs have rights to the territories they have always occupied. These territories are the West Bank and the Gaza Strip. Israelis argue that they own it by conquest according to the results of the Six-Day War.

When the British bailed out and left the United Nations with the task of administrating the division of the Palestinian territory, the suggestion was to create two states, with both sides sharing Jerusalem. The global expectation was that the United Nation's ruling would calm the situation and promote peace among these war-torn nations. However, history shows that this was not accomplished.[17]

To this day, Israel has not followed the ruling of the United Nations. Both Israelis and Palestinians missed a great opportunity to demonstrate to the world their firm belief in the Fatherhood of God and the brotherhood of humanity. Not to mention the countless fields of learning that would be shared mutually by such a social fusion.

"It is very clear that Israelis have settled in to lands that Palestinians call home and believe that its their right to live there. Palestine at the other hand wants its land back and world leaders have not been able to do anything to settle the long standing issue between the two parties. Thousands of people have died and the killing continues while the world looks the other way. There is a simple solution to all this and that is to go by what the United Nations says and even by the 1995, 1998 agreement signed by the two sides. [A] hand full of people on both sides doesn't want peace and are fully happy with the feud that has been running for years."[18]

Despite the rulings of the international community, Israel continues to do things their way. "Israel justifies its violation of international law [the Fourth Geneva Convention and other international laws governing military occupation of foreign territory] by claiming that the West Bank and the Gaza Strip are not technically 'occupied' because they were never part of the sovereign territory of any state. According to this interpretation, Israel is but an 'administrator' of territory whose status remains to be

---

15 Ibid., p. 170.
16 Bennis, "What Has Been the Role of the UN in the Israel-Palestine Struggle," Trans Arab Research Institute, http://1ref.us/22.
17 The Learning Network, "Nov. 29, 1947 | U.N. Partitions Palestine, Allowing for Creation of Israel," *The New York Times*, (accessed January 23, 2014).
18 "Who Owns Gaza Strip," MaybeNow, http://1ref.us/41.

determined. The international community has rejected this official Israeli position and maintained that international law should apply in the West Bank and Gaza."[19]

During the 1948 Arab-Israeli war, the Gaza Strip was conquered by Egypt and it became the sovereign territory of Egypt. Having full knowledge of this, Israel has continued the settlements to this day. Israel should put a stop to this territorial intrusion if there is to be any hope of peace in the Middle East. Israel claims that they own the land by virtue of biblical promise, but they are not working together with their neighbors to resolve the issues at hand.

In Genesis 17, long before the birth of Ishmael or Isaac, God promised Abraham that He would give to his seed, and all who were born in his household, the land of Canaan (verse 6). Ishmael was the firstborn son of Abraham in his household. According to the biblical promise, he was also heir to the promise. However, even though he was Abraham's firstborn, he was not the heir of the Promise—Isaac was. Notwithstanding, God blessed both of Abraham's sons. If Ishmael the illegitimate was heir of the promise made to Abraham, how much more would Isaac, the legitimate son have right also to the land of promise?

God promised Canaan to the Jews. It was their disobedience that provoked their expulsion (Lev. 26:32–46). It was God's intention after the birth of Isaac that both he and Ishmael would grow up together in their father's household. It was understood that both their descendants would be heirs of the Promised Land. However, Sarah had other ideas, and Ishmael was sent away.

Years later, with no pomp or ceremony, Isaac and Ishmael, side by side, buried their deceased father in the cave of Machpelah in Mamre (Gen 25:9). According to Hebrew tradition, Isaac and Ishmael did not wait until their father was dead to attend to his funeral. They came together while he was yet alive and spent the last days with him and with each other. Previous to this funeral service, there was bad blood between Isaac and Ishmael. However, it appears that the two brothers were reconciled by the death of their father since they both attended to his burial. Surely their descendants can find a way to live together under the canopy of a two-state solution.

The road is hard, but the destination is clear—a secure state of Israel and an independent prosperous Palestine. Peace is not an easy thing to orchestrate, and it must come from the Israelis and Palestinians, since they are the ones who must live near each other. They must be the ones to reach a workable agreement and stick to the guidelines outlined by both sides. It was Nelson Mandela who said, "For to be free is not to merely cast off one's chains, but to live in such a way that respects and enhances the freedom of others."[20] If we want to be free, are we willing to extend the same freedom to others?

Conflict of interest has led some Jewish insurgents to peddle the idea that God abandoned Ishmael who had absolutely no favor whatsoever in His eyes. A blunter version of this vernacular would be that the innocent child will pay eternal consequences for the sins of his or her parents. This is not in step

---

19 "Primer on Palestine, Israel and the Arab-Israeli Conflict," Middle East Research and Information Project, http://1ref.us/3b.
20 Mandela, "Nelson Mandela Quotes," Brainy Quote, http://1ref.us/33.

with God's character. If the unrighteous receives mercy through the sacrifice of Jesus, then surely the innocent will be the recipient of more abundant mercy. The sins of the parents visit the children unto the third and fourth generation. It is equally true that His mercies reach back much farther to the children of those who love Him and serve Him (Deut. 5:9, 10). I believe God's intention was, and still is, to have both Jews and Palestinian Arabs live together in Palestine. Both ethnicities should embrace this divine mandate and begin getting use to the idea. As was discussed, Canaan (Palestine) was promised to both Ishmael and Isaac. Therefore, it would seem that both of them have rights to occupy Palestine. This is God's promise, and God keeps His promise.

Acceptance that the descendants of Ishmael are rightful joint heirs to the land of Canaan is perhaps the solution to the dilemma in the Middle East. When the followers of Judaism, Islam, and Christianity—the three greatest faiths that descended from Abraham—rise up and live out the true meaning of their creed, to love God and love their neighbor as themselves, a two-state solution would become a reality.

Consider what would happen if Palestinian Arabs were applying the Golden Rule when dealing with their Jewish brothers and sisters. They would not have waited for the Balfour Declaration to create a homeland for the Jews who were victims of European anti-Semitic persecution. They would have taken the initiative themselves. By the same token, doing to the Palestinian Arabs as they would do unto themselves would have compelled the Jews to be content with what was miraculously given back to them. It is within reason that they could not expect to be given all the pre-exile territory they possessed, some of which was now occupied by Palestinian Arabs. Israel was bent on regaining every inch of their pre-exile territory. They trod where the Golden Rule would not tread—they began bulldozing down the homes of the Palestinian Arabs and began the infamous settlements that continue to the present day. This is a blatant violation of the Golden Rule. This is not how love operates. Love builds bridges, not walls. Love extends the hand of friendship, not violence. Unfortunately, fear, selfishness, and hate often squeeze out love. For the peace of the world, it is the hope of billions that in the end love will prevail.

The Road Map to Peace in the Middle East

Palestinians, at all cost, should avoid the shifting duplicity politics employed by their predecessor, Yasser Arafat. The Israeli-Palestinian talks in the Norwegian capital of Oslo culminated on September 13, 1993, in the signing of the Declaration of Principles on Interim Self-Government Arrangement. This provided for Palestinian self-rule in the entire West Bank and Gaza Strip for a transitional period not to exceed five years. During this interim period, both parties were to negotiate a permanent peace settlement. The Oslo accords enabled the Palestinian Liberation Organization (PLO) to achieve in one swoop what it failed to attain through many years of violence and terrorism.[21]

The Palestinian movement was at its lowest ebb a decade after serious damage was inflicted to the PLO's military structure in Lebanon. Yet Israel sought out the Palestinian organization to establish

---

21 "Text: 1993 Declaration of Principles," BBC News, http://1ref.us/3o.

a real political and military presence. Speaking from both sides of his mouth, Yasser Arafat became notorious for his double-dealing tactics and maneuvers. His ultimate objective was never a two-state solution. He was bent on replacing the state of Israel with a Palestinian state.[22] Arafat set out to build an extensive terrorist infrastructure in flagrant violation of the accords. He refused to disarm the militant religious groups Hamas and Islamic jihad as required by the treaties. He tactfully approved the murder of hundreds of Israelis by these groups.[23]

Anyone with a sound knowledge of the history of the Middle East would attest that surrounding Arab states compounded the problem. These nations and jihadist radicals, distanced from the immediate region, the foremost of which is Iran, are recalcitrant in denying the statehood of Israel. According to Karsh, there was a time when Arabism and Islam were fully synonymous, but those days have long since ended. Islam has traveled far from its Arabian origins to become a thriving universal religion. It boasts of a worldwide community of believers of whom Arabs are but a small minority. It is of noticeable importance that the quest for Allah's empire has passed from the monarchs to political activists and ideologues known as Islamists. The jihadists, unlike the monarchs, had "little interest in the deeper inculcation of Islam's precepts in their Muslim subjects, let alone in spreading Allah's message beyond the House of Islam."[24] These political activists patterned themselves after Islam's early conquerors and aspired not only to become the millenarian kingpin of the Middle East, but for the entire world. Hell will freeze over before Islamist states recognize the statehood of Israel.

History, the sole guardian of bipartisanship, identifies Great Britain among those who instigated the fiasco and political quagmire in the Middle East. Israel was an artificial alien entity created by British imperialism and implanted in the midst of Palestine. This would be the Trojan horse that would stampede, divide, and weaken Arab nationalism. This political ambition backfired, and now Britain has taken a back seat and the United States is leading the charge, when it should be the other way around.

"Years after the 1948 war, Nasser openly admitted to an American official that while he and his fellow officers had been 'humiliated' by the Israelis during the 1948 war, their main grievance was directed 'against our own superior officers, other Arabs, the British and the Israelis—in that order.' 'Britain is the main cause of the Palestine catastrophe,' he said in a public speech in Alexandria in December 1953. 'The Arabs tend to forget this fact and blame Israel and the Jews, but they are afraid to acknowledge that Britain is the cause.' In line with this thinking, both Nasser's published war memoirs and *The Philosophy of the Revolution* are conspicuously free of anti-Israel invective."[25]

In November of 2005 the birthplace of Christ was sealed off from Jerusalem by a wall just in time for Christmas. This wall cuts some four to six kilometers into the West Bank. While many nations sympathize with Israel in protecting itself from jihadist radicals, this wall cuts deep into Palestinian territory, creating devastating social effects of freedom of movement within their land and crippling

---

22 Karsh, *Islamic Imperialism: A History*, p. 186.
23 Ibid., p. 187.
24 Ibid., p. 212.
25 Ibid.

the local economy. More than two thousand years after the birth of Christ, Bethlehem, the cradle of Christianity, is barricaded by a wall. It is the largest infrastructure project in Israel with a price tag to match. The United Nations estimates that the projected cost of the wall will exceed $1 billion. If it continues on its present course, the wall will eventually extend to more than 430 miles in length. This is more than four times the length of the Berlin Wall.

It is ironic that sixteen years after the fall of the Berlin Wall Israel built another wall. Abraham Lincoln said, "Those who deny freedom to others deserve it not for themselves, and, under a just God, cannot long retain it."[26] If this statement holds, then Israel's hands are not clean in the Middle-East conflict. "Even at the height of the Oslo peace process, Israel more than doubled the number of Jews it moved to live in the West Bank, raising fundamental questions among the Palestinians as to whether Israel was more interested in grabbing land than peace."[27] The voice of the church must not be silent on these matters. It should continue clamoring for "judgment [to] run down as waters, and righteousness as a mighty stream" (Amos 5:24, KJV).

"The Israeli people, a people subjected to appalling persecution by the Nazi regime should know exactly the pain and suffering inflicted upon families from years and years of mental and physical oppression …, social isolation, mass killings and other methods used to deny them their right to existence."[28]

It is hard to understand how the international community, in particular the United States, can stand by and condone by their silence this inhumane debauchery. Perhaps the reason is because the 2009 United States Congress was comprised of a historic number of forty-five Jewish lawmakers (thirteen senators and thirty-two representatives).[29] Considering that the percentage of Jews as an ethnic group in America is only a little more than 2 percent of the overall population, this number is staggering.

If ownership of Palestine is determined by the United Nations, then the disputed territories of Golan Heights, the West Bank, and the Gaza Strip are Arab-Palestinian territories. On November 29, 1947, the United Nations General Assembly voted to partition Palestine into two states, one Jewish and one Arab. However, history is the reliable witness that every nation that invades another nation rules over it until it is overthrown. If conquest is the title deed to Palestine, then Israel, by virtue of the conquest of the famous Six-Day War in 1967, is its sovereign ruler.

Of course, for those of us who believe in the Word of God, Palestine, otherwise known as Canaan, belongs to whom God promised it. Therefore, it belongs to both the sons of Abraham—Isaac, representing the Jews, and Ishmael, representing the Arabs.

Prime Minister Benjamin Netanyahu alluded to the biblical tie of these two nations in remarks at a meeting in Washington, D.C., on September 2, 2010, with Secretary of State Hillary Rodham Clinton

---

26 Lincoln, "Search Collections," Smithsonian American Art Museum, http://1ref.us/31 (accessed January 27, 2014).
27 McGreal, "Obama: Halt to New Israeli Settlements Is in America's Security Interests," *The Guardian*, http://1ref.us/36.
28 Sabella, "The Wall Around Bethlehem," Global Ministries, http://1ref.us/3h.
29 Lieberman, "New Congress Has Record Number of Jews," The Jewish Daily Forward, http://1ref.us/30.

and Palestinian Authority President Mahmoud Abbas. He said, "In the first book of the Bible, the book of Genesis, there is a story of how two brothers in conflict—brothers, Isaac and Ishmael—joined together to bury their father Abraham, our father, the father of our two peoples. Isaac, the father of the Hebrew nation, Ishmael, the father of the Arab nation, joined together at a moment of pain and mutual respect to bury Abraham in Hebron.

"I can only pray, and I know that millions around the world, millions of Israelis and millions of Palestinians and many other millions around the world, pray that the pain that we have experienced—you and us—in the last hundred years of conflict will unite us not only in a moment of peace around a table of peace here in Washington, but will enable us to leave from here and to forge a durable, lasting peace for generations. Shalom. Salaam. Peace."[30]

It is my prayer that the descendants of two brothers reconciled by the death of their father could surely find a way to live together in peace.

---

30   Netanyahu, "Remarks With Israeli Prime Minister Benjamin Netanyahu, and Palestinian Authority President Mahmoud Abbas," Benjamin Franklin Room, Washington D.C., September 2, 2010.

Chapter 14

The Fifth World

Empire

Overview

This chapter answers tough questions about the fifth world empire. Will it be a coalition of the nations of Europe led by the United States? Will the day come when a freedom-loving country, a veritable fortress of religious liberty, will become a persecuting power? What do the two beasts of Revelation 13 have to do with the final demolition of capitalism? You will be shocked to discover who is sitting on almost all the gold in the world and what this sinister religious-political power will do with it to enforce the observance of Sunday as a day of worship.

Spiritual Winter in America

Jesus' return is imminent. And as we approach the end of the world, it is only fitting that the final events of earth's history will be carried out by one of the most powerful and influential nations on earth.

The United States of America could be called the United States of paradoxes. Students can sneak drugs, guns, and spiritualism into school, but they cannot take their Bibles. The founding fathers prayed for guidance before signing the Declaration of Independence, yet prayer is banned from public schools. Man has walked on the moon, but there are certain neighborhoods on United States soil where men are afraid to tread. We talk about human rights, but abortions claim the lives of more than 1 million babies every year.[1] During the Christmas season, people sing about peace on earth good will toward men, but then someone turns around and opens fire at a mall, killing innocent shoppers. We allow almost 21,000 people around the world to die from starvation every day,[2] a problem that could be solved by spending

---

1 "U.S. Abortion Statistics," Abort73.com, http://1ref.us/3s.
2 "World Hunger Statistics," Statistic Brain, http://1ref.us/3y.

The Fifth World Empire

50 billion dollars a year, when Americans spend 100 billion dollars a year gambling, not to mention billions of dollars spent on entertainment and other luxuries.[3]

When presidents have the audacity to lie under oath, desecrate hollowed national memorials, indulge in sexual imprudence, and manipulate intelligence to start a war, we are outraged. When CEOs cheat the system, juggle the numbers, cook the books, and are the perpetrators of all manner of atrocious financial frauds, people are shocked, speechless, bemused, and bewildered. Yet, the collective opinion, legally supported by the government, is that personal morality is somehow separated from work. Rape is punishable by law, yet with the click of a button one can look at pornography on the Internet and mentally rape the man or woman on the screen.

Americans seem to have discovered all the answers, but not the Answer! They know much more about the how-to but very little about the what-for. They are long on pleasure but short on purpose. The more money they generate in the stock markets, the more unsatisfied they are with life. They seek more pleasure, but easily become bored.

In the midst of all this gloom and doom, there is good tidings of great joy, "In the days of these kings [our days] the God of heaven will set up a kingdom which shall never be destroyed" (Dan. 2:44).

In the Days of These Kings

In a dream from God, which is recorded in Daniel 2, Nebuchadnezzar, king of Babylon, saw a tall magnificent statue. Its head was of pure gold, its chest and arms were silver, its thighs were of brass, its legs of iron, and its feet were part iron and part clay. In his dream the king saw a huge boulder strike the statue at its feet. The entire statue was pulverized and blown away like chaff in the wind. Daniel proceeded to interpret the dream, telling the king that the kingdom of Babylon was the head of gold and the first kingdom to rule the world. However, contrary to public opinion, the universal impact of the Babylonian kingdom was not foreseen as perennial and unending.

Represented by the chest and arms of silver, another inferior world empire would emerge after Babylon. This was the kingdom of the Medes and Persians. The prophet Daniel envisaged that there would be a third kingdom—Greece—represented by brass. This world kingdom was followed by a fourth that was as strong as iron. This was the kingdom of Rome.

This biblical narration accurately reported the course of history well in advance to it actually unfolding. These passages are biblical eschatology at its best. They allow the reality of the end to return to the present, shaping it for the glory of God. This is a merciful act of God that affords us the unique opportunity to position ourselves on the right side of history. In like manner that the Bible predicted, through the prophet Daniel, only four successive kingdoms ruled the world.

And according to Scripture, never again will the world come under the rule of one man or nation. Rome was the last of such empires. Daniel went on to explain that the iron kingdom would be divided. It would be broken up into ten kingdoms represented by the ten toes of the statue. These ten kingdoms

---

[3] "What Would It Cost to End Poverty," Conspiracy of Hope, http://1ref.us/42.

and the modern nations of Europe will never be reunited permanently under the rule of one nation according to the prophecy of Daniel 2: "And in that you saw the iron mixed with common clay, they will combine with one another in the seed of men; but they will not adhere one to the other, even as iron does not combine with pottery" (verse 43, NASB).

"They will not adhere to one another." These seven words have collided with the political ambitions of every would-be dictator since the Caesars. These seven words are the reason for history's uncanny repetitious saga, as one man and woman after the other, aspiring to rule the world, has gone down in defeat. Daniel goes on to explain, "In the days of those kings the God of heaven will set up a kingdom which will never be destroyed, and that kingdom will not be left for another people; it will crush and put an end to all these kingdoms, but it will itself endure forever" (verse 44, NASB).

"In the days of those kings," the nations of Europe, God will intervene. The Lord Jesus will appear in the skies and to His kingdom there will be no end. Here is something the postmodern mind that views biblical truth with suspicion can grapple with. History confirms that every single aspect of the prophecy of Daniel 2 has been fulfilled to the letter, all except for the last aspect, which has to do with the coming of Christ and the establishment of His unending kingdom.

The book of Revelation gives us additional insight to the prophecies of Daniel. Revelation 13 unfolds a panoramic view of the end-time events that will climax with the final destruction of capitalism. Let's examine the two beasts that are presented in Revelation 13. The first, which has seven heads and ten horns (verses 1–10), represents papal Rome. Being more precise, the seven-headed beast represents Satan working through seven successive world powers. These nations have taken an oppositional stance against God's truth and His people down through the ages. "The prophet, using a literary figure called 'synecdoche,' which names the whole for the part, presents the whole beast in order to refer especially to the seventh head—the papacy."[4] This power, the union of church and state, became a reality during the Middle Ages. Cloaking her political ambitions with a pious aura, this religious political juggernaut, a fusion of the sacred with the profane, played havoc with humanity's God-given freedom. Those who resist and oppose will be persecuted (Rev. 13:5–7).

The second lamblike beast is a fitting description of the United States of America (Rev. 13:11–18). In the Old World, church and state were glued together as one and the same. Here is a new form of government with two lamblike horns—the peaceful separation of the two powers of government and religion. Without a doubt the United States has been a freedom-loving country, a veritable fortress of religious liberty. Roger Williams spoke out against magistrates enforcing their personal religion. To escape arrest, he fled to the wilderness, living with the Indians. He later bought land from the Indians and established a new colony dedicated to religious liberty. He called the new settlement Providence, which today is the capital of Rhode Island. Jews, Catholics, and Quakers were welcomed as citizens in full and regular standing. America's democratic spirit is well represented by the metaphoric innocence of the lamblike beast. The philosophy of complete separation of church and state and its high regard

---

4 Chaij, *Preparation for the Final Crisis*, p. 96.

for individual liberties the likes of religious liberty, has made the United States the mecca for all the oppressed from the global community.

Papal Rome Empowered by America

Undisputedly, this prophecy presents a rather strange paradox. According to the prediction, this lamblike nation will discard its gentle manners and speak like a dragon, working in conjunction with papal Rome. It is written in Revelation 13:11, 12: "And I beheld another beast coming up out of the earth; and he had two horns like a lamb, and he spoke as a dragon. And he exerciseth all the power of the first beast before him, and causeth the earth and them which dwell therein to worship the first beast, whose deadly wound was healed."

The Perfect Economic Storm

A perfect economic storm is brewing on the political horizon. An improved economy is the sure path for the re-election of any United States president. It is easy to see why some believe that the calculated strategy of certain politicians is to purposefully crash the economy by balancing the national budget on the social conscience of the American society. It is common knowledge that such actions would produce a domino effect.

Most Americans are working for a meager salary, and as we discussed in a previous chapter, many rely heavily on public assistance programs. If the economy tanks and these programs are done away with, millions of people will be faced with economic conditions that will strangle them. Consumption will slow down dramatically. And if there is no consumption, the economy will crash. It is no surprise that the United States economy is collapsing as predicted in James chapter 5. The world economy draws its life from the United States economy. A dying system of capitalism in the United States will also mean death to the global economy.

As you are reading this, you may wonder why Congress isn't doing anything to prevent an economic collapse, but it would appear that they don't care since at least 50 percent of all congressional members are millionaires![5] This is what has led some to the conclusion that such actions are intentional. The collapse of the United States economy would become the Trojan horse some ambitious politicians hope to mount and gallop into the White House.

The love of money is the universal language that all mankind speaks eloquently. Notwithstanding, "all things work together for good to those who love God" (Rom. 8:28). The re-election of world leaders is never in the hands of their constituencies; it is in the hands of God. He is the One who sets up and removes kings: "I will not take the whole kingdom out of his hand, because I have made him ruler all the days of his life for the sake of My servant David, who I chose because he kept My commandments and My statutes" (1 Kings 11:34).

---

5   Lipton, "Half of Congress Members Are Millionaires, Report Says," *The New York Times*.

If we look to Bible prophecy, the crash of the global economy will mark the beginning of the end of the world, and God will prepare to set up His eternal kingdom, regardless of what the leaders of this earth think or do.

Collapse of United States Economy

Any attempt to fix the broken United States capitalistic economy, be it individually or collectively, will most likely be futile. Its global collapse is imminent. "There are not many, even among educators and statesmen, who comprehend the causes that underlie the present state of society. Those who hold the reins of government are not able to solve the problem of moral corruption, poverty, pauperism, and increasing crime."[6]

It is difficult to fathom that the United States economy has been declining since around 1976. Many Americans, especially Baby Boomers who have the most to lose if social security is done away with because of lack of funds, are in denial and find it hard to admit that the United States is no longer as prosperous as it used to be. A brief study of the history of the four basic types of money reveals why America is not as solvent financially as is portrayed to the world. There is commodity money (land and gold), receipt money, fractional money, and fiat money.

In the beginning of the monetary system, the golden rule was, "He who has the gold rules." The gold prospectors would store their gold, commodity money, in high security vaults, thus protecting their assets from being stolen. With the passage of time, people who acquired gold brought it to the gold icons for it to be safeguarded in their vaults. A receipt was given to the clients by which they could retrieve their deposited gold. Of course, they had to pay a fee for this service. This was called "receipt money." The receipt was as good as the gold. It was not practical to walk around with huge quantities of gold to be exchanged for land, clothing, food, and other commodities of life, and there came a time when only gold receipts were circulated as real money.

The gold icons noticed that their clients were not taking out the deposited gold. Instead they were using the receipts for their transactions. Instead of having the gold sit there doing nothing, the banker would lend it (via receipts) to those who were desirous of borrowing at a fixed interest rate. The bank would keep only a fraction of the entire gold money deposited and would lend out the remaining portion. The money in the bank was called "fractional money." A bank would crash if all the receipt holders demanded their deposited gold at the same time. In reality, the banks did not have much gold money. What they had is known as "fiat money," money that is worthless with no gold to back it up.

In today's financial industry, the same process is still in effect. This worthless conglomeration of receipt/fractional/fiat money circulates because the government enforces it via the Federal Reserve, which was founded in 1913. Here is the conclusion of this matter. There is sufficient receipt money for all Baby Boomers to retire. The problem is that there is no "gold" in the bank to back it up. The million-dollar question is who has the original gold, which has been accumulating over the centuries, for which

---

6   White, *Testimonies for the Church*, vol. 9, p. 13.

receipt monies were issued? It is certainly not in the United States Federal Reserve. The identity of this global gold icon will now be disclosed.

The Image to the Beast

The global financial meltdown is more marked in Europe. There is a strong possibility that a temporary fixing of the collapsed global economy will come from the Vatican, which is headquartered in Rome. For centuries this religious-political machine, exempt and autonomous from the scrutiny and audit of the global economy, has been storing its wealth in gold. The Vatican could be sitting on vaults that contain gold accumulated over centuries. "The Catholic church is the biggest financial power, wealth accumulator and property owner in existence. She is a greater possessor of material riches than any other single institution, corporation, bank, giant trust, government or state of the whole globe. The pope, as the visible ruler of this immense amassment of wealth, is consequently the richest individual of the twentieth century. No one can realistically assess how much he is worth in terms of billions of dollars."[7]

It is within the reach of reason that a collapsed global economy, rehabilitated by the Vatican, could force all nations to bow to the dictates of the pope and the Roman Catholic Church, thus forming an image to the beast. The image would honor the Vatican for bailing out the worldwide failing economy. It is of noticeable importance that the text from Revelation indicates that other nations in the world make the image to honor the beast.

America's role in this drama, acting the part of a supporting cast member and speaking as a dragon to enforce the dogmas of papal Rome, is supported in the Hebrew Scriptures: "And he [lamblike beast, which is America] deceives those who dwell on the earth by those signs which he [America] was granted to do in the sight of the beast, telling those who dwell on the earth to make an image to the beast who was wounded by the sword and lived." (Rev. 13:14). It is of noticeable importance that the text from Revelation indicates that other nations in the world make the image to honor the beast. Once the image is made, America will enforce it, speaking "like a dragon" in the process (verse 11).

A Vatican that has rehabilitated the global economy will be empowered to make heavy demands. One such demand could be to enforce Sunday observance, arguing that failure to observe Sunday as the Sabbath is the reason for the collapsed economy. Those who observe the Sabbath will be persecuted. How is it that America, a freedom-loving country and a defender of religious liberty over the years, will become a persecuting power to enforce Sunday observance? Could it be that this nation will go against its Constitution and enforce religious practices to honor the beast or the Vatican for bailing out a collapsed economy?

"When the leading churches of the United States, uniting upon such points of doctrine as are held by them in common [Sunday observance, immortality of the soul, postmillennial coming of Jesus, dispensational theology, etc.], shall influence the state to enforce their decrees and to sustain their

---

7 "Is the Vatican Rich Enough to Wheel Power over G20 Nations?" The Truth and the Truth Alone, http://1ref.us/2p (accessed May 17, 2011).

institutions, then Protestant America will have formed an image of the Roman hierarchy, and the infliction of civil penalties upon dissenters will inevitably result.... The 'image to the beast' represents that form of apostate Protestantism which will be developed when the Protestant churches shall seek the aid of the civil power for the enforcement of their dogmas."[8]

The Sunday Laws

Baby Boomers are not tickled about being duped by the United States social security retirement program. It is easy to see why the Vatican, now the leading economic force in the world, will be positioned to call for the passing of universal Sunday laws. The justification will be that such an action is the solution to the global economic recession.

"The dignitaries of church [Catholicism] and state will unite to bribe, persuade, or compel all classes to honor the Sunday. The lack of divine authority will be supplied by oppressive enactments. Political corruption is destroying love of justice and regard for truth; and even in free America, rulers and legislators, in order to secure public favor, will yield to the popular demand for a law enforcing Sunday observance."[9]

Baby Boomers are currently the most populous segment of the United States population. The political landscape of the twenty-first century is theirs to shape. They have the political voice and vote to enforce Sunday observance. How then could it be justified that a nation whose Constitution advocates for separation of church and state suddenly entertain a motion to enforce religious laws?

Here are some valid justifications. First of all, more and more Protestant churches in America are erasing the thin line that separates church and state. Their argument is forceful and compelling. State intrusion on the church is unconstitutional, but church intrusion on the state is acceptable and gaining momentum. Secondly, there is a growing trend in America that gives cause for concern. As was previously mentioned, Protestant churches in America are linking themselves to each other through doctrines held in common. Read the following insightful words:

> By the decree enforcing the institution of the papacy in violation of the law of God, our nation will disconnect herself fully from righteousness. When Protestantism shall stretch her hand across the gulf to grasp the hand of the Roman power, when she shall reach over the abyss to clasp hands with spiritualism, when, under the influence of this threefold union, our country shall repudiate every principle of its Constitution as a Protestantism and republican government, and shall make provision for the propagation of papal falsehoods and delusions, then we may know that the time has come for the marvelous working of Satan and that the end is near.[10]

---

8   White, *The Great Controversy*, p. 445.
9   Ibid., p. 592.
10 Ibid., p. 445.

Thirdly, the economic prowess of the Vatican will leave this nation with no alternative but to play the game by its rules and demands. Lastly, the Baby Boomers have the vote. It is understandable why they would readily bend over backwards to hold on to their retirement that is slipping away, for "the love of money is the root of all evil" (1 Tim. 6:10, KJV).

Chapter 15

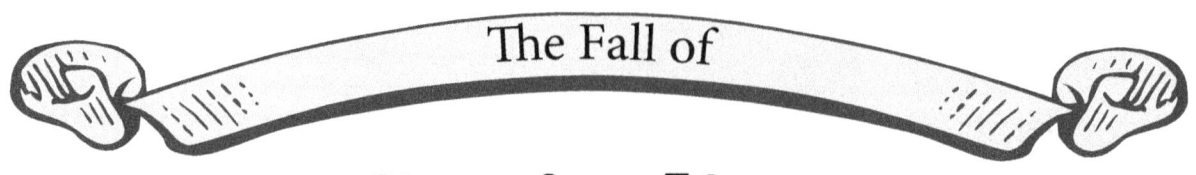

The Fall of Capitalism

Overview

"The Bible foretells the coming of a very different social order—a restored world in which economic activity and priorities will be handled very differently and more fairly than they are today."[1] This chapter presents a detailed description of the end of capitalism as we know it today. The revolutionary thought is that God's kingdom will be established when capitalism is destroyed. On that day, the prediction of Karl Marx will finally come to pass. Capitalism, which contained the seeds of its own destruction, will collapse giving rise to a new world order controlled by God. Then shall come to pass the saying, "One nation under God and the blood-stained banner of Immanuel, indivisible, with liberty and justice for all."

God Taking Control

"Like the stars in the vast circuit of their appointed path, God's purposes know no haste and no delay.... [Divine] Providence had directed the movements of nations, and the tide of human impulse and influence, until the world was ripe for the coming of the Deliverer"[2] the first time, and the same is true of Jesus' second coming, which will mark the end of capitalism. Jesus is not coming to take sides. He is coming to take over! One of the greatest promises of the Bible is that God is not a cosmic regulator or a deific designer who merely designs natural laws, sets them in motion, and then abandons planet earth to the mercy of destiny. He will intervene on behalf of the oppressed when there is no one to stand against the oppressors.

---

1   Welch, "Everymoney: Capitalism, Democracy and Global Wealth: Part 3," *Vision*, http://1ref.us/12.
2   White, *The Desire of Ages*, p. 32.

He intervened in the antediluvian society when "the wickedness of man was great in the earth, and that every intent of the thoughts of his heart was only evil continually" (Gen. 6:5). It was God Himself who allowed for the destruction of the earth by a flood.

He intervened for the oppressed Jewish nation throughout the annals of history. Pharaoh tried to drown them, but they would not be drowned. Ancient enemies tried to exile them, but they would not be exiled. Haman tried to hang them, but they would not be hanged. Nebuchadnezzar tried to burn them, but they would not be burned. Hitler tried to gas them, but they would not be gassed. Modern enemies tried to push her into the sea, but she would not be pushed. How have God's people been able to survive all these atrocities? God has been with them and protected them from total destruction.

Looking at American history, God intervened on behalf of the African slaves in the cotton fields of the South. How were blacks in America able to crawl from the slave pits of segregation and sit at the table of brotherhood in the palaces of their masters? The same God who is always on the side of the oppressed was with them.

God will intervene on behalf of the working class under capitalist oppression. Recently, there has been a radical shift to the right in American politics. The working class and the most vulnerable of society—youth, children, women, and seniors—find themselves under heavy oppression by the political innuendos from the extreme right. Under the disguise of small government and reducing the deficit, galling laws are enacted that will cut key public funding the rich can live without. The poor and working classes are not so fortunate. There is talk about cutting social security, eliminating funds for public education, operating fewer public hospitals, and doing away with minimum wage.

The quest to balance the national budget on the social conscience of society may work for a short time to the detriment of the most vulnerable of society, but in the end God will triumph and will redeemed His followers who have suffered under a heavy load. God, the undisputed heavyweight Champion for the oppressed, is positioning Himself to establish His kingdom on earth, which will last forever. It is not necessary to organize demonstrations the likes of Occupy Wall Street, pitting the 99 percent against the 1 percent. There is no necessity to send a text message to God to update Him on the recent developments. He is with us and is aware of what is going on. Let us stand still and see the salvation of God.

The End of Capitalism

The prophetic reality is that there is a sense in the air of a foreboding doom that stalks and haunts apostate capitalism. Its final demise makes way for a radically new order. The apostle James describes how capitalism's robust global trading system will come to a violent end:

> And a final word to you arrogant rich: Take some lessons in lament. You'll need buckets for the tears when the crash comes upon you. Your money is corrupt and your fine clothes stink. Your greedy luxuries are a cancer in your gut, destroying your life from within. You thought you were piling up wealth. What you've piled up is judgment. All the

workers you've exploited and cheated cry out for judgment. The groans of the workers you used and abused are a roar in the ears of the Master Avenger. You've looted the earth and lived it up. But all you'll have to show for it is a fatter than usual corpse. In fact, what you've done is condemn and murder perfectly good persons, who stand there and take it. (James 5:1–6, MSG)

Capitalism is overbearing, sinister and entrenched in greed and skullduggery. Global revolts against such a system are unmistakable signals that it is the greatest stumbling block along the road to universal peace and lasting prosperity! Corporate capitalism, as it is, will be destroyed before God sets up His kingdom. There is no human power on earth that can destroy this empire of corporate ruthlessness. God will be left with no alternative but to strike the economic nerve of capitalism and bring about the final destruction of this economic system devised by human hands. He will intervene and arrange for its destruction.

When the stock market crashes, merchants and stockbrokers will all be forced to take early and permanent retirements. Prophet Ezekiel warns that on the day capitalism ends "all hands shall be feeble, and all knees shall be weak as water…. They shall cast their silver in the streets, and their gold shall be removed: their silver and their gold shall not be able to deliver them in the day of the wrath of the Lord" (Ezek. 7:17, 19, KJV). Money will have no value. All bank foreclosures will be placed on permanent hold. There will be no more need for taxes and tax breaks for the wealthy elite or for the working class. There will be no more battles in Congress to extend unemployment benefits. Politicians will get the budget cuts they panted after. There will be no more money for wars. The national debt will find its final resting place in the section of bad debts in the cosmic ledgers of eternity.

The good news is that which will be a dark moment for some will be cause for celebration for others. For the first time in history, the most powerful nation on earth, within whose borders resides the bastion of capitalism, will be backed into an undesirable corner over which she has no control. It will finally bow out to God's eternal kingdom. The Bible envisages a kingdom that will restore all things (Rev. 20:1–6). On that day it will be said, "O tower of the flock, the strong hold of the daughter of Zion, unto thee shall it come, even the first dominion" (Micah 4:8, KJV).

After the earth is destroyed and wickedness is gone forever, all humankind will live together under the benevolent leadership of God. His kingdom "will be a new social order, with a foundation of moral and ethical principles guaranteed to resolve the inherent inequity, selfishness and greed of the best system that man has constructed."[3] The foremost difference with today's world and God's kingdom is that all forms of violence and wars will be eradicated and God's principles will be understood and practiced, for those who are selfish will have long been destroyed by the brightness of the second coming of Jesus (see 2 Thess. 2:8 and Rev. 11:18). It is odd that much of the Christian world has turned its back on the

---

3   Welch, "Everymoney: Capitalism, Democracy and Global Wealth: Part 3," *Vision*, http://1ref.us/12.

biblical truth of the second coming of Jesus. "An overwhelming tide of secular thinking has all but eclipsed it,"[4] but the Bible is clear—it will happen, regardless of if people are ready or not.

What the New World Is Not

Consider what God's kingdom will be like. It will be "a world where the good of all is the overriding preoccupation of a government that is not corrupt and self-serving."[5] A society that is free of all forms of racial distinctions, in which all the redeemed will live side by side in peace and equality. "The nature of today's economic activity will be brought under the kind of direction that will ensure the good of all. Human nature will at last be subdued, and God's moral code will become the norm. As people are given the opportunity to understand what God requires of them and they are enabled to make the right choices with the help of a renewed mind, permanent changes will result (Isaiah 2:2–3). Cooperation and collaboration will transform all relationships, as people are convinced that their own interests must be balanced with concern for others. [The norm of capitalism will be reversed, and it will no longer be who has what, but who gets what.] The reality of a future world unified through sound spiritual values is laid out in the major and minor prophets (see, for example, Jeremiah 31:33–34; Zephaniah 3:9)."[6]

"The earth shall be full of the knowledge of the Lord" *(Isa. 11:9, KJV)*. Under the current capitalistic economy, the working class works harder than anyone else in the system only to see what should have been a just compensation wage go into the pockets of the rich. Unlike capitalism's regime, in God's kingdom its inhabitants will not "build and another inhabit; they shall not plant and another eat" (Isa. 65:22, 23). Poverty, which could have long been relieved from the entire globe, will be gone forever. In God's kingdom, both Islam and Judaism will occupy the heavenly Canaan as joint heirs of the promise God made to Abraham. On that day the all God's followers, who will have come from the various religions of the world, will rise up and live out the true meaning of their creed, which is to love God and their neighbor as themselves. In that land, "Every man [will become] is an heir of the legacy of dignity and worth."[7] True lasting peace at finally come to the Middle East, and the sons of Abraham will inhabit the land together.

The prophet Isaiah spoke these words almost 3,000 years ago, "Nation shall not lift up sword against nation, neither shall they learn war anymore" (Isa. 2:4). In God's kingdom there will be no lower, middle, upper, and working classes. The wealth of the land will be equally available to all its citizens. The redeemed, spurred by pure consciences and an inherent concern for the fortunes of others, will live together in an orderly and beneficial manner.

In God's kingdom, our morality will be the product of our nature and not our reason. Competition will give way to love, the true "glue" that will bind its citizens together. There will be no greedy transactions sparked by self-interest in the land where we will never grow old. "Democracy will be replaced

---

4   Ibid.
5   Ibid.
6   Ibid.
7   King, *A Knock at Midnight: Inspiration from the Great Sermons of Reverend Martin Luther King, Jr.*, p. 86, 87.

by [a] benevolent theocracy."[8] No longer will funds from heavy taxes be levied against us by the "king" to charter our sons and daughters off to war. Big business will no longer see the environment as just another resource to be used for profit making. "All economic activity, whether the provision of energy, the harvesting of fish from the ocean, food from the land, or wood of the forest, will be in harmony with what the environment can sustain."[9] It will not be to sustain avarice and greed. "They shall not hurt nor destroy in all My holy mountain" (Isa. 11:9). There is more good news about this kingdom. All the abortion clinics will be closed. No longer will innocent lives be selfishly snuffed out of existence under the pretext of birth control.

The Blood-stained Banner

The flag that will be flown from the canopy of God's eternal kingdom will not be the Union Jack of the British, the Tricolor of France, or the Star-Spangled Banner. It will not be the Star of David or the Belizean flag that Marion Jones carried, along with the American flag, when she won her first gold medal in the Summer Olympics in Sydney, Australia, in honor of her mother, to which she was "punished" by American society for paying tribute to a third-world country through their treatment of her during the anti-doping investigation. The flag will be the blood-stained banner of Jesus Christ, and all the injustices of life, including the ones I have experienced similar to Marion Jones, will disappear.

Even though we face difficulties on this earth, we should not lose hope. "Weeping may endure for a night, but joy comes in the morning" (Ps. 30:5). Remember, the darkest hour of human struggle will soon turn into the first hour of sweetest victory. Faith is about to adjourn the assemblies of hopelessness and will bring new light into the chambers of pessimism. Napoleon Bonaparte was quoted as saying the following, "Alexander, Caesar, Charlemagne and I myself have founded great empires; but upon what did these creations of our genius depend? Upon force! Jesus alone founded His empire upon love, and to this very day millions will die for Him."[10]

Global revolts in a world punctuated by free enterprise sends a singular message. The entire globe clamors for a hybrid system that emerges from those noble principles that constitute the best of both capitalism and socialism. This is the system in which the government levels the playing field and plays by the same rules. The good news is that God is positioning Himself to establish such a kingdom on earth that will last forever. Divine providence is putting it together at the rate of one day and one person at a time. Then shall come to pass the saying, "One nation under God, indivisible, with liberty and justice for all."[11] Until then, we move forward, ever trying to make things better on this earth while keeping our eyes focused on the hope that Jesus will return and peace and happiness will reign in His eternal kingdom.

---

8   Welch, "Everymoney: Capitalism, Democracy and Global Wealth: Part 3," *Vision*, http://1ref.us/12.
9   Ibid.
10 "'Jesus Alone Founded His Empire Upon Love'–Napoleon Bonaparte," Christ Centered Teaching, http://1ref.us/1w.
11 "The Pledge of Allegiance," Historic Documents, http://1ref.us/1x (accessed January 23, 2014).

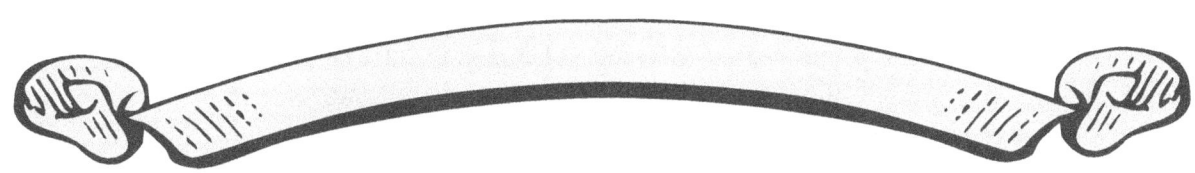

Bibliography

"10 Great Quotes About the Value of Education." Everest University Online. http://1ref.us/1p (accessed March 25, 2014).

"2011 London Anti-cuts Protest." Wikipedia. http://1ref.us/1q (accessed January 23, 2014).

"A Friend of the Capitalists." Thr@ll. http://1ref.us/t (accessed March 3, 2014).

"Amish and the Plain People." LancasterPA.com. http://1ref.us/1r (accessed March 25, 2014).

"Acceptance Speech at Nobel Peace Prize Ceremony." The Martin Luther King, Jr. Research and Education Institute. http://1ref.us/1s (accessed April 2, 2014).

Adams, Gordon. "After Katrina Fiasco, Time for Bush to Go." The Baltimore Sun. http://1ref.us/1t (accessed September 25, 2009).

Akkerman, J. R. "The Graphic Gospel: Preaching in a Postliterate Age." Abstract. Asbury Theological Seminary.

Allinson, Jamie. "How Did Capitalism Come Into Being?" Socialist Worker. http://1ref.us/17 (accessed April 14, 2011).

"America's Paradox: Broke Government, Rich Corporations." Business Insider. http://1ref.us/v (accessed October 29, 2013).

Anderson, Kerby. "Wealth and Poverty—A Biblical Perspective." Probe Ministries. http://1ref.us/1u (accessed March 25, 2014).

Angelou, Maya. Brainy Quote. http://1ref.us/14 (accessed April 28, 2011).

"Arab-Israeli Conflict." Wikipedia. http://1ref.us/1v (acessed April 5, 2014).

"Arab Spring." Wikipedia. http://1ref.us/1y (accessed August 25, 2011).

"Are Federal Workers Overpaid?" FactCheck.org. http://1ref.us/1f (accessed September 16, 2013).

Bacon, Francis. Brainy Quote. http://1ref.us/1z (accessed January 27, 2014).

"The Balfour Declaration of 1917." History Learning Site. http://1ref.us/20 (accessed January 23, 2014).

Beattie, Andrew. "The History of Capitalism: From Feudalism to Wall Street." Investopedia. http://1ref.us/15 (accessed March 4, 2014).

Beinin, Joel, and Lisa Hajjar. "Palestine, Israel and the Arab-Israeli Conflict—A Primer." Middle East Research & Information Project. http://1ref.us/21 (accessed April 7, 2014).

Bennis, Phyllis. "What Has Been the Role of the UN in the Israel-Palestine Struggle." Trans Arab Research Institute. http://1ref.us/22 (accessed January 23, 2014).

Blond, Phillip. "The End of Capitalism As We Know It?" David Lindsay's blog. http://1ref.us/23 (accessed March 20, 2014).

Bolton, Robert. *People's Skills: How to Assert Yourself, Listen to others, and Resolve Conflicts.* New York: Simon and Shuster, 2001.

Bratcher, Dennis. "Ba'al Worship in the Old Testament." The Voice, Christian Resource Institute. http://1ref.us/24 (accessed July 3, 2011).

Buchanan, Patrick J. "Enron and the Decline of Capitalism." The American Cause. http://1ref.us/25 (accessed May 22, 2009).

"Capitalism Destroys the Family, Admits BUSINESS WEEK Magazine." Reprinted from *The People* March 25, 1995. http://1ref.us/26 (accessed January 23, 2014).

Chaij, Fernando. *Preparation for the Final Crisis.* Nampa, ID: Pacific Press Publishing Association, 1966.

"Criminal Justice Fact Sheet." NAACP. http://1ref.us/27 (accessed September 16, 2013).

Dalmia, Shikha. "Pope Francis Shouldn't Bite the Hand That Feeds the Catholic Church." Washington Examiner. http://1ref.us/19 (accessed January 23, 2014).

"Deforestation in Brazil." Wikipedia. http://1ref.us/28 (accessed January 23, 2014).

Desilver, Drew. "Black Unemployment Rate Is Consistently Twice that of Whites." Pew Research Center. http://1ref.us/29 (accessed April 23, 2014).

Dobbs, Lou. "Dobbs: Congress Stiffs Working Americans." CNN.com. http://1ref.us/1c (accessed September 8, 2009).

Du Bois, W. E. B. "The Talented Tenth." In The Negro Problem. New York: James Pott and Company, 1903.

Dzado, Natalie. "2010 Average Life Expectancy by Gender, Race, and Country." Suite. http://1ref.us/2a (accessed February 3, 2011).

"Eastern Europe Proverb Quotes." Thinkexist.com. http://1ref.us/2b (accessed April 17, 2010).

Einstein, Albert. Brainy Quote. http://1ref.us/2c (accessed January 23, 2014).

"Federal Minimum Wage Increase for 2007, 2008, & 2009." Labor Law Center. http://1ref.us/1b (accessed March 10, 2014).

"Federal Minimum Wages Rate, 1955–2013." Infoplease. http://1ref.us/2d (accessed July 6, 2010).

"Foreclosure Statistics." NeighborWorks America. http://1ref.us/2e (October 19, 2009).

"The Gettysburg Address." Abraham Lincoln Online. http://1ref.us/10 (accessed January 21, 2014).

Gandhi, Mahatma. "Mahatma Gandhi Quotes." Thinkexist.com. http://1ref.us/1l (accessed September 22, 2009).

Gilbert, Dennis. *The American Class Structure*. New York: Wadsworth Publishing, 1998.

Goldberg, Jonah. *Liberal Fascism: The Secret History of the American Left From Mussolini to the Politics of Change*. New York: Broadway Books, 2007, 2009.

———. "Obama, the Postmodernist." USA Today, August 5, 2008.

Goolsbee, Austan. "Democratizing Capitalism." Democratic Leadership Council. Blueprint Magazine, July 22, 2006.

Gottschalk, Keith. "A U.S. View: Democracy, Bought and Paid For." Rabble.ca. http://1ref.us/y (accessed April 23, 2014).

Gray, Louise. "Era of Cheap, Easy Oil Is Over, Warns Study." The Telegraph. http://1ref.us/2g (accessed January 27, 2014).

Halper, Daniel. "Report: U.S. Spent $3.7 Trillion on Welfare Over Last 5 Years." The Weekly Standard. http://1ref.us/2h (accessed June 19, 2014).

Harden, Blaine. "Africa's Diamond Wars." The New York Times. http://1ref.us/2i (accessed March 25, 2014).

———. "Africa's Gems: Warfare's Best Friend." The New York Times. http://1ref.us/2j (accessed March 25, 2014).

Hargreaves, Steve. "15% of Americans Living in Poverty." CNN Money. http://1ref.us/2k (accessed January 23, 2014).

"Henry Ford's $5-a-Day Revolution." Ford. http://1ref.us/1d (accessed January 25, 2014).

"The History of Welfare." Welfare Information. http://1ref.us/1o (accessed February 25, 2011).

"Homosexuality." Wikipedia. http://1ref.us/2l (accessed April 3, 2014).

"How Many Calories Do I Need a Day?" Fitwise.com. http://1ref.us/1j (accessed September 8, 2009).

"How Many Households are in the US?" Wiki Answers. http://1ref.us/2m (accessed September 25, 2013).

"Inspiration." Project True. http://1ref.us/2n (accessed April 1, 2014).

"Intelligence Quotes." DecentQuotes.com. http://1ref.us/2o (accessed April 1, 2014).

"Is the Vatican Rich Enough to Wheel Power over G20 Nations?" The Truth and the Truth Alone. http://1ref.us/2p (accessed May 17, 2011).

Jackson, David, and Aamer Madhani. "Obama to Raise Minimum Wage for Some Federal Workers." USA Today. http://1ref.us/2q (accessed April 23, 2014).

Jackson, Jesse. "1984 Democratic National Convention Address." American Rhetoric. http://1ref.us/2r (accessed August 14, 2006).

"'Jesus Alone Founded His Empire Upon Love'–Napolean Bonaparte." Christ Centered Teaching. http://1ref.us/1w (accessed April 8, 2014).

Johnson, Paul. *The Quotable Paul Johnson: A Topical Compilation of His Wit, Wisdom and Satire*. Edited by George J. Marlin, et al. New York: Farrar, Straus and Giroux, 1994.

Karsh, Efraim. *Islamic Imperialism: A History*. New Haven/London: Yale University Press, 2007.

———. "What Occupation?" Commentary. July–August 2002.

"The Kibbutz." Jewish Virtual Library. http://1ref.us/13 (accessed June 2, 2009).

King, Martin Luther Jr. *A Knock at Midnight: Inspiration from the Great Sermons of Reverend Martin Luther King, Jr.* Edited by Clayborne Carson and Peter Holloran. New York: Warner Books, Inc., 1998.

King, Martin Luther Jr. "Quotation #32615 from Classic Quotes." The Quotations Page. http://1ref.us/o (accessed July 2, 2007).

Knight, Alex. "Anti-Capitalism Goes Mainstream: Review of 'Capitalism: A Love Story.'" End of Capitalism. http://1ref.us/2t (accessed October 19, 2009).

———. "Part 1. Is This the End of Capitalism?" End of Capitalism. http://1ref.us/2u (accessed March 31, 2014).

———. "Part 2. What is Capitalism?" End of Capitalism. http://1ref.us/11 (accessed March 3, 2014).

———. "Part 3: Why Is It Breaking Down?" End of Capitalism. http://1ref.us/2v (accessed March 31, 2014).

———. "Part 5. Conclusion: The World We Are Building." End of Capitalism. http://1ref.us/2w (accessed March 31, 2014).

———. "Review of 'You Call This a Democracy? Who Benefits, Who Pays, and Who Really Decides?'" End of Capitalism. http://1ref.us/x (accessed June 3, 2009).

Konczal, Mike. "Economists Agree: Raising the Minimum Wage Reduces Poverty." Wonkblog. The Washington Post. http://1ref.us/2x (accessed January 29, 2014).

Korten, David. "The Betrayal of Adam Smith—Excerpt." Living Economies Forum. http://1ref.us/18 (accessed September 29, 2009).

Kyongsuk, Anselm. *The Solidarity of Others in a Divided World: A Postmodern Theology After Postmodernism.* New York: T & T Clark International, 2004.

Lach, Alex. "5 Facts About Overseas Outsourcing: Trend Continues to Grow as American Workers Suffer." Center for American Progress. http://1ref.us/2y (accessed April 23, 2014).

Laffin, John. *The PLO Connections.* London: Corgi Books, 1983.

Larson, David. "Capitalism: What Were Its Moral Strengths and Weaknesses? Part 1." Spectrum. http://1ref.us/r (accessed February 13, 2014).

"Liberation Theology." Wikipedia. http://1ref.us/2z (accessed April 23, 2014).

Lieberman, Brett, and Rebecca Spence. "New Congress Has Record Number of Jews." The Jewish Daily Forward. http://1ref.us/30.(accessed January 27, 2014).

Lincoln, Abraham. "Search Collections." Smithsonian American Art Museum. http://1ref.us/31 (accessed January 27, 2014).

Lipton, Eric. "Half of Congress Members Are Millionaires, Report Says." The New York Times, January 9, 2014.

Locker, Phillip, and Dan DiMaggio. "Global Capitalism = Global Warming—The Case for Socialism." Socialist Alternative. http://1ref.us/32 (accessed June 1, 2009).

Mandela, Nelson. "Nelson Mandela Quotes." Brainy Quote. http://1ref.us/33 (accessed September 8, 2013).

"Martin Luther King Jr. Quotes." Goodreads. http://1ref.us/34 (accessed April 2, 2014).

Maxwell, John C. *Developing the Leader Within You.* Nashville, TN: Thomas Nelson Publishers, 1993.

McBratney, Sam. "The Rise of the Bourgeoisie." Lisburn.com. http://1ref.us/16 (accessed March 31, 2011).

McGreal, Chris, and Rory McCarthy. "Obama: Halt to New Israeli Settlements Is in America's Security Interests." The Guardian. http://1ref.us/36 (accessed November 20, 2009).

McKenna, Josephine. "Pope Francis Says Wasting Food Is Like Stealing From the Poor." The Telegraph. http://1ref.us/1n (accessed January 27, 2014).

Meakin, John. "The Achilles' Heel of Capitalism." Vision. http://1ref.us/s (accessed January 21, 2014).

Mody, Ashoka, and Franziska Ohnsorge. "G7 Consumption Growth: Implications for Recovery and Global Imbalances." Vox. http://1ref.us/1g (accessed January 23, 2014).

Mother Teresa. "Mother Teresa of Calcutta (1910–1997)." The Holy See. http://1ref.us/n (accessed June 2, 2009).

MSNBC.com staff. "Record Number of Americans Living in Poverty." NBCNEWS.com. http://1ref.us/1h (accessed September 18, 2010).

"NAD Remuneration Scales for January 1, 2005." Seventh-day Adventist Church. http://1ref.us/37 (accessed January 21, 2014).

Netanyahu, Benjamin. "Remarks With Israeli Prime Minister Benjamin Netanyahu, and Palestinian Authority President Mahmoud Abbas." Benjamin Franklin Room, Washington D.C., September 2, 2010.

Nichol, Francis D., editor. *Seventh-day Adventist Bible Commentary.* Vol. 7. Hagerstown, MD: Review and Herald Publishing Association, 1980.

Norman, Bruce R. *Bridging the Gap: Reaching the Internet Generation: An Evangelistic Strategy for Reaching the Postmodern Generation.* AdventSource, 2003.

Orchard, Steven. "Who Crippled Capitalism?" Vision. http://1ref.us/40 (accessed April 2, 2014).

"The Pledge of Allegiance." Historic Documents. http://1ref.us/1x (accessed January 23, 2014).

Polecolaw. "How Much Does Welfare Cost?" Newsvine. http://1ref.us/38 (accessed January 27, 2014).

"Postmodernism." United Church of God. http://1ref.us/39 (accessed March 31, 2014).

"President Obama Holds Press Conference." The Washington Post. http://1ref.us/3a (accessed June 23, 2014).

"Primer on Palestine, Israel and the Arab-Israeli Conflict." Middle East Research and Information Project. http://1ref.us/3b (accessed April 7, 2014).

"Profit Over People: The Immorality of Capitalism." Daily Kos. http://1ref.us/3c (accessed January 27, 2014).

Rank, Mark R. "Poverty in America Is Mainstream." The New York Times. http://1ref.us/3d (accessed January 25, 2014).

"Religion in the United States." Wikipedia. http://1ref.us/3e (accessed April 2, 2014).

Robbins, Duffy. *This Way to Youth Ministry: An Introduction to the Adventure.* Grand Rapids, MI: Zondervan Publishing House, 2004.

"Ronald Reagan Quotes." NotableQuotes. http://1ref.us/3f (accessed April 2, 2014).

Ronsvalle, John and Sylvia. "Church Member Giving in Recession Years: 1974, 1980, 1982 and 1990." Empty Tomb, Inc. http://1ref.us/3g (accessed April 23, 2014).

Sabella, Zack Bernard. "The Wall Around Bethlehem," Global Ministries, http://1ref.us/3h (accessed April 8, 2014).

"Separation of Church and State - The Metaphor and the Constitution." AllAboutHistory.org. http://1ref.us/3i (accessed February 13, 2014).

"The Seventh-day Adventist Church: Its Beliefs and Practices." ReligiousTolerance.org. http://1ref.us/3j (accessed June 4, 2009).

Sheedy, Nick. "The 'Pro-Life' and 'Pro-Choice' Position on Abortion." The Nolan Chart. http://1ref.us/3k (accessed January 27, 2014).

Shin, Laura. "The 85 Richest People in the World Have as Much Wealth as the 3.5 Billion Poorest." Forbes. http://1ref.us/1k (accessed April 28, 2014).

Siddiqi, Samana. "Statistics on Poverty and Food Wastage in America." SoundVision.com. http://1ref.us/1m (accessed October 19, 2009).

Smith Jr., Chuck. *The End of the World As We Know It.* Colorado Springs, CO: Waterbrook, 2001.

Souri, Ranjit. "How U.S. Food Aid Policies Perpetuate Poverty." India Currents. http://1ref.us/1i (accessed September 7, 2009).

"Stewardship of the Environment." Seventh-day Adventist Church. http://1ref.us/3l (accessed January 21, 2014).

Stewart, Connie. "Income Gap Between Rich and Poor is Biggest in a Century." Los Angeles Times. http://1ref.us/3n (accessed October 3, 2013).

"Text: 1993 Declaration of Principles." BBC News. http://1ref.us/3o (accessed January 27, 2014).

Thomson, Alice. "Why the Recession Is a Blessing in Disguise." Bangladesh News. http://1ref.us/3p (accessed January 27, 2014).

"Tony Benn Biography." Biography Online. http://1ref.us/z (accessed November 8, 2013).

Tracinski, Robert. "The Moral Basis of Capitalism." The Center for the Advancement of Capitalism. http://1ref.us/p (accessed January 21, 2014).

"The Tragedy of Palestine." The Hashemite Kingdom of Jordan. http://1ref.us/3q (accessed April 7, 2014).

"The True Identity of the So-called Palestinians." Myths, Hypotheses and Facts Concerning the Origin of Peoples. http://1ref.us/3r (accessed June 5, 2009).

"U.S. Abortion Statistics." Abort73.com. http://1ref.us/3s (accessed April 8, 2014).

Waldron, Travis. "One in Four American Workers Will Be in Low-Wage Jobs for the Next Decade." Think Progress.http://1ref.us/3t/ (accessed June 19, 2014).

Welch, William. "Everymoney: Capitalism, Democracy and Global Wealth: Part 1." Vision. http://1ref.us/q (accessed February 14, 2014).

———. "Everymoney: Capitalism, Democracy and Global Wealth: Part 2." Vision. http://1ref.us/u (accessed May 31, 2009).

Welch, William, and John Meakin. "Everymoney: Capitalism, Democracy and Global Wealth: Part 3." Vision. http://1ref.us/12 (accessed May 31, 2009).

"What Are the Annual Earnings for a Full-time Minimum Waged Worker?" Center for Poverty Research. http://1ref.us/1e (accessed September 16, 2013).

"What Is Capitalism?" World Socialist Movement. http://1ref.us/w (accessed March 3, 2014).

"What Would It Cost to End Poverty." Conspiracy of Hope. http://1ref.us/42 (accessed July 3, 2014).

White, Deborah. "Barack Obama's Controversial '06 Speech on Religion & Politics." About.com US Liberal Politics. http://1ref.us/3u (accessed April 2, 2014).

White, Ellen G. *The Desire of Ages*. Mountain View, CA: Pacific Press Publishing Association, 1898.

———. *Education*. Mountain View, CA: Pacific Press Publishing Association, 1903.

———. *The Great Controversy*. Mountain View, CA: Pacific Press Publishing Association, 1911.

———. *Testimonies for the Church*. Vol. 9. Mountain View, CA: Pacific Press Publishing Association, 1909.

"Who Is the Real Capitalism?" Waspadafurqon's Blog. http://1ref.us/3v (accessed June 2, 2009).

"Who Owns Gaza Strip." MaybeNow. http://1ref.us/41 (accessed April 7, 2014).

Wilsdon, Tony. "How Capitalism Breeds Poverty." Committee for a Workers' International. socialistworld.net. http://1ref.us/1a (accessed March 10, 2014).

Wilstein, Matt. "Dr. Ben Carson Calls Obamacare 'Worst Thing Since Slavery' at Values Voter Summit." Mediaite. http://1ref.us/3w (accessed April 23, 2014).

Wolfe, Alan. One Nation After All. New York: Putnam Penguin Books, 1998.

Wolff, Richard. "Capitalism Hits the Fan." AlterNet. http://1ref.us/3x (accessed May 25, 2009).

"World Hunger Statistics." Statistic Brain. http://1ref.us/3y (accessed January 27, 2014).

"Youth Voting Stats." Young Democrats of America. http://1ref.us/3z (accessed April 1, 2014).

We invite you to view the complete
selection of titles we publish at:

www.TEACHServices.com

Scan with your mobile
device to go directly
to our website.

Please write or email us your praises, reactions, or
thoughts about this or any other book we publish at:

P.O. Box 954
Ringgold, GA 30736

info@TEACHServices.com

TEACH Services, Inc., titles may be purchased in bulk for
educational, business, fund-raising, or sales promotional use.
For information, please e-mail:

BulkSales@TEACHServices.com

Finally, if you are interested in seeing
your own book in print, please contact us at

publishing@TEACHServices.com

We would be happy to review your manuscript for free.

www.ingramcontent.com/pod-product-compliance
Lightning Source LLC
Chambersburg PA
CBHW081841170426
43199CB00017B/2807